A WEALTH OF PRAISE FOR HYRUM SMITH AND *THE 10 NATURAL LAWS OF SUCCESSFUL TIME AND LIFE MANAGEMENT*

"Our values, relationships, and objectives can be accomplished, and with more inner peace and happiness and with a higher degree of self-satisfaction, by subscribing to and understanding natural laws the way Hyrum has well described in his book."
  —Jerry C. Atkins,
    Chairman, President, and CEO, Skywest Airlines, Inc.

"Anyone who invests the time to read the book will find it hugely profitable. It's also a fun, thoroughly enjoyable read. . . . Your methods have made MCI a more successful company."
  —Timothy F. Price,
    President, Business Services, MCI Telecommunications Corporation

"I thought I had heard or read everything pertaining to time management—boy, was I wrong. . . . The tools, the exercises, the concepts, and the philosophies that you present in the book are real, new, and useful. . . . It's great."
  —John R. Felone, co-author, *The Fall of the House of Hutton*

"TEN NATURAL LAWS is the consummate work in time management, *and* a blueprint for happiness. . . . This book will change your life!"
  —Marc and Vicki Sorenson, National Institute of Fitness

"Hyrum Smith adds practical advice about how to use truths to make our business and personal lives more satisfying and more productive. Every time I pick the book up, I learn something new."
  —M. Anthony Burns,
    Chairman, President, and CEO, Ryder System Inc.

"Offers a blueprint that will help assure improvement. The 10 laws start with taking personal responsibility for behavior and end with life-enriching insights."
  —Bruce L. Christensen,
    President and CEO, Public Broadcasting Service

The

10

NATURAL LAWS OF SUCCESSFUL TIME AND LIFE MANAGEMENT

Proven Strategies for Increased Productivity and Inner Peace

HYRUM W. SMITH

WARNER BOOKS

A Time Warner Company

Warner Books, Inc., 1271 Avenue of the Americas, New York, NY 10020

W A Time Warner Company

Printed in the United States of America
First Printing: January 1994
10 9 8 7 6 5 4 3

LIBRARY OF CONGRESS CATALOGING-IN-PUBLICATION DATA

Smith, Hyrum W.
    The 10 natural laws of successful time and life management :
proven strategies for increased productivity and inner peace / Hyrum
W. Smith.
        p.   cm.
    ISBN 0-446-51741-0
    1. Time management.   2. Stress management.   3. Life skills.
I. Title.   II. Title: Ten natural laws of successful time and life
management.
HD69.T54S6   1994
640'.43—dc20   92-51037
                                                                   CIP

Book design by Giorgetta Bell McRee

To my wife
Gail

The shadow by my finger cast
Divides the future from the past.
Behind its unreturning line,
The vanished hour, no longer thine.

Before it lies the unknown hour,
In darkness and beyond thine power.
One hour alone is in thine hands,
The now on which the shadow stands.

—Poem inscribed on a sundial
at Wellesley College

CONTENTS

ACKNOWLEDGMENTS

No effort of teaching and communication is ever a solo performance, and this book is not an exception to that natural law. Many people have shaped its content and the direction of my life and thinking over the years, and at the outset I need to express to them my sincere and heartfelt gratitude.

Richard I. Winwood, one of the founders of Franklin Quest Co., is deserving of special mention. Dick and I go back a long way, and I don't believe there is another person on the planet that I am closer to than Richard. My respect and love for him is very hard to describe, but without his influence in my life, the company would not exist nor would this book.

To Lynn Robbins, Dennis Webb, Bob Bennett, and Greg Fullerton, the other founding members of Franklin Quest, I express sincere appreciation for their personal impact on my life and their contributions to the success of what we have accomplished together. Arlen B. Crouch, Jay L. Atwood, and Val John Christensen, who serve on the executive committee of Franklin Quest Co., have also contributed much and have directed us to the successful point at which we find ourselves now in corporate America.

I would also mention Marion D. Hanks, a deeply spiritual man and powerful communicator who has played an integral role in my life for many years. He has been a very serious mentor in shaping my thought processes, my inner convictions, and my ability to communicate them to others. To him I express a sincere love and appreciation.

Deep appreciation is expressed to Jerry Pulsipher, who assisted me in writing this book and, along with Kurt Hanks, helped refine the Reality Model and many other key intellectual concepts taught in Franklin's seminars. Jerry has helped me translate concepts and thoughts I have felt strongly about into written form, and I extend heartfelt thanks and appreciation as a colleague and sounding board. Without Jerry, the book literally would not have come to pass.

A special acknowledgment needs to be made to my wife, Gail, and my children—Glenna, Stacie, Sharwan, Joseph, Rebecca, and Jacob—who have been such a source of support and strength and encouragement through the last twenty-five years. Gail has been an absolute rock through some major financial difficulties early in our life together and in the fragile beginnings of Franklin Quest Co. Without her, there is no question that none of this would have happened. To Gail and my six wonderful children, I say thank-you and express my love.

A book like this is always the combined effort of many others who have helped to clarify the principles and processes of personal development. My own thinking has been strongly impacted by many of these individuals, some of whom I have been privileged to know personally and others who have influenced me through their writings and the spoken word. Many of them are acknowledged in the text, but I want to give special recognition to Alan Lakein, Alec R. MacKenzie, Charles R. Hobbs, and James W. Newman. The clarity of their thinking has made my own task immeasurably easier.

Thanks too to many individuals who for many years have encouraged me to put these things into printed form. I especially note the contribution of Ken Shelton, who first suggested the overall organization of the book, assisted us in finding a publisher, and kept after me to see that I got the book written.

Many others helped shape the manuscript. Roger Terry provided valuable assistance in the book's initial draft, and Joann Davis, executive editor at Warner Books, gave consistent encouragement and suggestions that gave clarity and polish to the finished manuscript. Thanks, too, to Carol Force, my executive assistance at Franklin Quest, who helped keep all the loose ends together.

I would like to mention the many others at Franklin Quest Co. who have played a role in making this all possible, but space will not allow more than a blanket expression of appreciation to all of the Franklin Quest team who have brought us to this point in our venture. I feel that we have just dusted off the surface of what we can accomplish together and know that we have yet to accomplish many great things that will continue to make a difference in the lives of others.

—HYRUM W. SMITH
St. George, Utah
March 1993

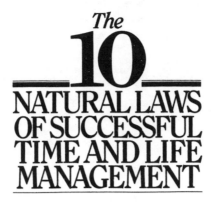

The 10
NATURAL LAWS OF SUCCESSFUL TIME AND LIFE MANAGEMENT

Why You Should Read
This Book

If you don't read anything else, read these few pages.

I often wonder why people buy books with titles like this. Perhaps the answer can be summed up in an experience I've repeatedly had teaching time management seminars all over the world.

At the beginning of each seminar, I ask participants, "Why did you come today?" The initial responses run something like: "Well, I want to be more productive." "My boss asked me to come." "I would like to spend more time with my family." "I would like to get more done in eight hours so I can get home earlier." "I would like to be less frustrated at work." "I want to reduce my stress."

However people state it, the responses generally come down to one very simple idea: *"I'm here because I want to feel better about myself and my life."* And the reason people want to feel better is because they sense that their lives are out of control: The things that matter most in life are too often hostage to the things that matter least. They have come to the seminar because they believe that managing their time more effectively will help them gain control, and that's true—but only to a point. The real solution—the way to "feel better"—goes beyond simply managing time more efficiently.

I recently came across an article and a couple of books that talk about an important part of this problem. According to a recent issue of *Time* magazine, we live in the age of "time famine." Life is getting more and more hectic. The daily treadmill is accelerating, and we have to run faster and faster just to stay in one place. People all across America are feeling the crunch. The demands of the competitive marketplace put such a premium on personal productivity that if you're not productive, you're out. The result is a tremendous pressure to perform, coupled with a sense of overwhelming insecurity about the future.

The increasing time demands of our careers are reflected in our personal lives as well. In his thoughtful book, *Time Lock*, Ralph Keyes describes our current condition as the time equivalent of gridlock on our highways. Our lives are so filled with things we *must* do or *should* do, let alone the things we *want* to do, that we feel trapped, literally unable to do anything.

In his book, *The Harried Leisure Class*, Staffan B. Linder points out the time demands placed upon us by the things we own or acquire. The purchase of a new boat or car or even a new book brings its own time requirement—time needed to learn how to use it or to maintain it or just to read it. Each new thing or person coming into our lives literally says to us, "Hey, spend time with me," and we do, even when we don't find much satisfaction in it. Paraphrasing the words of the old TV commercial, are you doing more now and enjoying it less? If you're like most people today, the honest answer is too often yes. Indeed, the pace and pressures of life have become so insane that people feel they're losing control of their lives.

Everyone wants to be in control. This is one of the most compelling desires of all human beings. There is no worse feeling than being out of control, sensing that other people or external circumstances govern what we do (and when and how we do it), feeling that we are puppets on a string, being yanked back and forth by forces over which we have no influence. In fact, psychologists have discovered that suicide is very often the ultimate quest for control: "The only thing I can control is whether I live or not." When something or someone else controls our lives, we are neither happy nor productive, and we don't experience inner peace. Unfortunately, peace, productivity, and happiness are three commodities that seem to be in short supply today, because people sense that they are not in control of their lives.

The focus of this book, then, is not exclusively on time management but on achieving *inner peace*—the transcendent feeling of fulfillment and well-being we all seek. Time management is only a set of skills and tools to help us more *efficiently* control the events of our lives. But efficient time management alone will never give us inner peace. Ralph Keyes correctly points out that "Timelock persists and gets worse despite the fact that time management concepts are widespread. . . . With their emphasis on getting more done in less time, too many approaches to managing time are more part of the problem than of the solution."

The secret to achieving inner peace lies in understanding our inner *core values*—those things in our lives that are most important to us—and then seeing that they are reflected in the daily events of our lives. In other words, doing a better job of managing our time is meaningless unless we are managing it to accomplish those things that are of greatest importance in our lives. That critical difference between simply managing our time and finding the fulfillment that comes from being in control of our lives is what this book is all about. And this simple concept—of making sure that our daily activities reflect our deepest core values—is the concept that has made all the difference in my own life. Let me illustrate.

On June 3, 1992, I found myself standing on the floor of the New York Stock Exchange with my wife and family to witness a singular event in our lives. It was the day that Franklin Quest Co., a company that had been given birth in my basement less than nine years earlier, was to become a publicly traded company on the New York Stock Exchange.

Earlier that morning we had been the guests of the Exchange, along with the other founders of the company, at a lovely breakfast. We were then taken down to the floor of the exchange to witness the stock come up on the big board for the first time.

After preliminaries involved in pricing the stock, a per-share offering price was established and a flurry of activity of buying and selling of shares of our company on the NYSE began. I looked up at the big board and there, for the first time, FNQ came across the ticker tape at $16.50. I can't begin to describe the emotions that flooded through my system. I stood there amid three thousand people scurrying on the floor of the Exchange, with my partners who had helped create the company standing around me, and wept like a baby.

My tears came not because of my own newly enhanced net worth because of the shares of the company that I owned. Rather, it was because of what we had done in such a short time by following some deeply held core values. What flooded into my mind were the vivid memories of the road that had brought us to this point in our lives— of shaky beginnings, of hundreds of nights spent in hotels, of those who believed with us and produced our products and seminars, and of those who bought the products and attended the training and wrote to tell us of its impact in their lives. But most of all, I realized that the company's success was living proof of the idea that following your inner values really works.

Somewhere early in my life, I can't remember exactly where or how, I developed the obsession that for some reason I was supposed to make a difference with my life. I once heard Winston Churchill speak, and in his remarks he indicated that he had a similar obsession. As I came to appreciate the impact Winston Churchill had not only on Great Britain but also the world, I realized he was indeed a person who made a differ-ence—for millions of people. So it was with my desire. From a young age, I have wanted to make a difference in people's lives. That has been a driving, compelling force inside me for a long time.

After graduating from college I discovered that I had abilities in selling. Eventually joining a national firm in the data processing business, I found myself at a relatively early age as senior vice-president of marketing and sales for the largest division in the company. During this period, I discovered that not only was I excited about selling, but that I also enjoyed teaching others how to sell and succeed. I discovered an ability to speak and motivate—skills that were in line with my obsession to make a difference in people's lives.

In February of 1978, my church contacted me and asked if I would be willing to take a three-year leave of absence to go to California and manage one of their missions. Because of my commitment to my church and my inner drive to make a difference, I and my family went to California and for three years worked with more than six hundred men and women who were doing full-time volunteer missionary service. During those three years, I honed my speaking and motivational skills and discovered that what I wanted to do most of all was to teach. I began looking at my options to move into teaching and quickly realized that I didn't have the credentials to teach in the academic world. If I was going to satisfy my desire to teach and make a difference, I would have to do it in the corporate world. After a great deal of thought and prayer, my wife and I determined that we would follow the road of teaching.

This was not an easy decision, especially in light of the fact that my former employers approached me a few months before our mission service was to end and offered me a very lucrative job in New York City as a senior executive of the firm. The offer was enticing, but I found myself saying, "Hyrum, if teaching is something you feel deep inside you are supposed to do, you'd better do it." By this time I had developed some pretty strong feelings about following what my inner values suggested I ought to do. So, we turned down that opportunity. Many of my former colleagues thought I was crazy. There were a few moments in the months to come when I wondered if that was not true as well. But that decision— to follow my inner governing values—was one of the pivotal decisions of my life.

In July 1981, my wife and I created a small seminar company. We called it Gem, Inc. for Golden Eagle Motivation, after another obsession I have had throughout my life—eagles. We initially developed two seminars, one on selling and another on personal improvement. Looking back more than a decade later, neither seminar was very good. But for one year, we beat our heads against the wall in an attempt to break into the seminar business in the corporate world. Through a small miracle in financing and some help from a very close friend, we were able to survive financially while we learned the seminar business and eventually moved into the area of time management training, working as an independent training consultant for a firm specializing in that field.

An old friend, Richard I. Winwood, also worked for the same firm, and together we began exploring better ways of teaching and implementing the principles of time management in the seminars we were teaching. Several years earlier, Dick had developed a simple but powerful model of value-based goal achievement called the Productivity Pyramid that resonated with my own feelings about following inner values. We began using the pyramid in our seminars and found that it had impact on others as well. We also identified the need for a special day-planning tool that would fit the principles and processes we were teaching more closely than any products then available on the market.

When it became evident that the training firm we were with was not interested in pursuing some of the directions we now felt strongly about, Dick Winwood and I, along with Lynn Robbins, Dennis Webb, and Greg Fullerton, created our own time management seminar firm, the company that would eventually become Franklin Quest Co. It was a pretty gutsy thing to do, as none of us had any money. But, we had a message we wanted to take to the world—a message we strongly felt would make a difference.

Working out of my basement, Dick and I started going out and scratching together what seminars we could. Lynn Robbins and Dennis Webb worked to create and refine our own day-planning tool, the Franklin Day Planner. We saw it as a modern embodiment of the "little book" Benjamin Franklin devised to schedule his time and focus on improving his efforts. We began teaching people about the Productivity Pyramid and how to use the Franklin Day Planner to help them bring their daily activities in line with their inner governing values. We asked them to use the system for twenty-one days, and then to write to tell us how it was working in their lives. As letters started to pour in, telling about significant changes in the lives of these people, we were even more convinced that we were on the right track and redoubled our efforts.

In those early days, we were fortunate to find some major corporate clients—Merrill Lynch, Citibank, Nike, Northern Trust Bank in Chicago—who liked what we were doing for their people and kept inviting us back. Within a year, we were teaching so many seminars that we began hiring additional consultants to sell and teach for us.

From those beginnings, this little company of ours has grown to where we are now teaching over twenty thousand people in live seminars every month. Well over two million people all over the world use the Franklin Day Planner. One of the largest web press operations in the western United States is kept busy around the clock to produce planners and associated products. We ship Franklin Day Planners to 133 countries, and now sell through more than twenty-five retail stores in shopping malls and shopping centers across the United States. Several hundred customer service agents handle toll-free telephone orders for products listed in our twice-a-year catalog mailings. Franklin Quest Co. now employs more than one thousand people in the Salt Lake City area alone, not to mention those in area offices and retail locations around the country and abroad. In 1993, Franklin Quest's gross revenues will exceed $160 million.

To me, the most exciting thing about this story is the impact that we are having in the personal lives of the people who go through our seminars and discover the magic of the Franklin Time Management System. At the Dow Chemical Company, for example, we taught our first seminar in January 1985. Since that time, we have trained more than twenty-five thousand white-collar professionals at Dow Chemical, and have developed a special edition of the Franklin Day Planner designed to meet some of the special needs of their company. Most of Dow's training is now done by in-house facilitators using a video we have specially prepared for them.

Dow has done two studies over the last four years to quantify the impact of the Franklin Quest training and the use of the Day Planner in their company. The first study was completed four years ago and the other was conducted within the last year. Both studies show that more than 90 percent of the people trained at Dow were still using their planners and that the average increase in productivity was more than 25 percent. These are chemists and engineers.

There are over three thousand corporations and government agencies now taking our training and using the Franklin Day Planners. We also conduct public seminars in over 170 cities to reach people who work for small businesses and the general public. Our own studies verify the fact that over 90 percent of those who go through our courses are still using their planners two and three years later. Why? *Because both the training and the tool work* for them. The principles we teach *do* give people better control over their lives. They experience the inner peace we talk about. They know what it is like to feel better—to be in control.

All of these things flooded over me as I stood on the floor of the New York Stock Exchange and realized that the dream was coming to fruition—that we *were* making a difference. Going public was only a beginning, giving us the financial capability to make that difference felt in the lives of an increasing number of people.

And we're going to continue to make a difference. We are taking our message to anyone who will listen. We are international now—with offices in London, Tokyo, Hong Kong, Taiwan, Canada, Mexico, Australia. We are moving as fast as we prudently can to get the message of control and inner peace to the world with easily understood training and tools that can be used by anyone.

Let me share an experience that suggests the potential power that the natural laws discussed in these pages can have in your life. An executive with the Merrill Lynch Corporation attended our seminar several years ago at their corporate training facility in Princeton, New Jersey, as part of the advanced training Merrill Lynch provides its brokers after their first year with the firm. A year after this gentleman had gone through the seminar he wrote me a four-page handwritten letter that, even as I think about it today, makes me emotional. In his letter he said something to this effect: "Hyrum, I went to your seminar a year ago in Princeton. It never occurred to me that what I do on a daily basis ought to be based on my governing values. I found that to be a very exciting idea. I came away from that seminar and identified my governing values, the things that really matter most to me. In the process of that introspection, I discovered that one of my governing values was a good life for my son. When I admitted that to myself, I also had to admit that I wasn't doing anything for my son. This past year, I decided I would dedicate my life to making a good life for my son."

He then described several fun things that he had done with and for his son. On the third page of this handwritten letter he said, "Hyrum, last week my son, eight years old, was killed in an automobile accident. I have experienced some real pain at the loss of my son. But I have to tell you that I have experienced no guilt. For the first time since your seminar, I realized what you were talking about when you discussed the idea and concept of inner peace." He then closed the letter by saying, "Hyrum, thank you."

I can't begin to tell you the impact that letter and many others like it has had on me. This man decided to do something about what really mattered to him. He did something about it and then went through a tragic loss. But, he didn't have to go through the guilt that many of us experience when we lose a loved one. Too often we find ourselves reflecting on all the things we should have done, or could have done, or ought to have done and we have all of the uncomfortable feelings that follow—all because we get so caught up in urgencies and in doing things that we think we have to do that the things that matter most tend to be overlooked.

I believe that the quest for inner peace—and the happiness that comes with it—is a life ambition of every person on the planet. Ultimately, we want to feel good about ourselves. We want to be excited to get up in the morning. We want to be in control of what can be controlled. The exciting thing is that this is not only possible—it is also doable. What you will discover in this book will help you do exactly that.

Why have the Franklin Time Management System and the Franklin Day Planner been so successful? Because they work! In thirty-six hours after going to our seminar or reading this book and implementing what you will learn, you will experience significant increases in control. I challenge you to read this book and do the twenty-one-day experiment that the book describes. Then you'll witness what it feels like to really be in control and to experience this magnificent thing—inner peace.

It has now been many months since that experience on the floor of the New York Stock Exchange, but I will never forget it. My family will never forget it. For me, it was the right decision not to take the lucrative job offer with the big company, but instead to go out on my own and struggle to do what my governing values were screaming at me to do. Franklin Quest, a company that is positively affecting the lives of thousands of people daily, is a result of a couple of people who decided to do what their values insisted they do.

I am not asking you to read this book and apply the ten natural laws taught here because I *think* they will work for you. I am asking you because I *know* they will help you gain control and inner peace. I have proved it myself. I know what it is like to get up in the morning knowing exactly where I am going, why, and how to get there. I know what it is like to have time to spend with my wife and children when I want to do it because everything has been accomplished and I am *in control* of things that are in my corporate world, in my family, in my church, in my avocations. I know what it is like to be able to say no because I am already committed to the hilt. I know what it is like to go to bed at night knowing that I have accomplished what really mattered to me that day and though I didn't get everything done that I would like to have got done, the things that were done were the

A's—the vital tasks, the things that really meant the most to me. It feels good.

Read the book. Do the twenty-one-day experiment. Write me a letter afterward and share with me what you have learned and how you feel. I'll respond to your letter. Discover the magic of inner peace.

What Are Natural Laws?

On March 14, 1992, I found myself riding a newly acquired horse. This was a very spirited, athletic animal trained to be a cutting horse. A cutting horse is specially trained by ranchers to separate a cow or steer from the herd. To anticipate or respond to a steer's movements, a well-trained cutting horse moves all by itself without any direction from the rider.

I soon discovered that my new horse would move all by itself even when no cattle were present. And not being an expert horseman, I was surprised when the horse suddenly decided to move without letting me know. Indeed, the horse moved so fast that I fell like a stone off its left side—only about a five-foot drop, but I landed so hard on my left shoulder that I broke my collar bone and five ribs, with one rib broken in three places. I lost my wind—thought I was going to die—and for about twenty minutes I was unable to move. As I lay there on the ground, gasping for breath, I found myself muttering, "The law of gravity is alive and well." Now, I may not understand *why* the law of gravity works the way it does, but I certainly understand *how* it works. I've had experience with it.

We're all aware that there are natural laws in the universe, even if we don't understand them very well. We've had experience with them. We're also aware that if we don't pay attention to them, if we don't take them seriously, we face predictable consequences. For instance, if we ignore the law of gravity or take it lightly, it will, you might say, have an impact on us. If we try to build a plane without understanding and applying the laws of aerodynamics, we will face predictable consequences. If we don't take into account the pertinent natural laws when we build a dam, disaster will follow. This is because natural laws are both immutable and consistent.

When I was doing a seminar at Citibank in New York several years ago, I asked the participants what a "natural law" is. I received the normal responses. A number even said, "The law of gravity."

"The law of gravity is an *example* of a natural law," I responded, "but how would you define a natural law?"

A gentleman raised his hand and said, "A natural law is a law that cannot be repealed." The more I thought about that, the more I realized what a wonderful definition he'd given.

We can get together and vote against the law of gravity, but our vote wouldn't make one bit of difference. If we then lined up on the top of a building and walked single file off the edge in defiance of that law, we'd be greasy spots on the pavement. The law of gravity would prevail. There is nothing we can do about a natural law. We can't repeal it, and we're crazy if we ignore it.

Let's Be Sure We Understand Our Terms

Before we get too far, you need to understand what I mean when I talk about natural laws. To me, **natural laws** are *fundamental patterns of nature and life that human experience and testing have shown to be valid. They describe things as they really are, as opposed to how we think they are or how we wish they were.* Whether we agree with them or not, these laws ultimately govern our lives and operate independent of our awareness or wishes. By becoming aware of them and working with them, we can live safely and successfully. If we ignore them or fight them, we will fail and make ourselves and others miserable.

Natural laws have always existed and been with us regardless of whether or not people have been aware of them. The natural laws governing the physical world, for instance, have affected human lives from the beginning of time. As we have come to understand these natural laws, we have developed sound and creative solutions to our cultural needs.

Immense dams, for example, are built on rivers to store water from wet months for use in dry months, to generate electricity, to stabilize the flow of rivers, prevent flooding, and to create recreational opportunities. These dams are carefully planned. In designing and building them, engineers take into account natural laws that govern such things as how water flows, how much pressure a certain volume of water exerts, how stable the ground is, how certain shapes can transfer weight and pressure to a canyon wall, and how heavy and strong concrete is. If these natural laws are respected in building the dam, it will stand and fulfill the purpose for which it was built. If these laws are ignored in planning and building the dam, the dam will likely burst, with disastrous results for those living below.

Similarly, we can put huge 747s in the air and safely fly people all over the world because we understand the laws of aerodynamics. We can take a beautiful symphony, transform it into digital codes, print those codes on a palm-size disk and then read and translate those codes back into the original sounds by laser and computer technology. Instead of hearing random electronic noises, we listen to a faithful reproduction of the symphony in our own living rooms—all because we understand certain natural laws.

Our *collective* understanding of certain natural laws is rather impressive. However, our *individual* understanding of such laws is usually much less impressive. For instance, you should not trust me to build a dam upstream from your neighborhood. I'm not an engineer, and I haven't learned those particular natural laws. I couldn't design a working aircraft either (except the paper variety), and I definitely couldn't build a CD player. In fact, my understanding of the natural laws that govern the physical environment doesn't stretch far beyond the law of gravity, which I understand all too well. There are other natural laws, though, that operate on an internal or interpersonal level. Some of these I understand well enough to share with you, because they have made a difference in my life. These natural laws can help us gain control of our lives, improve our relationships, increase our personal productivity, and experience inner peace.

Now you might ask, "What do natural laws have to do with gaining control of our lives? What do they have to do with productivity or happiness or inner peace?" Well, in addition to the natural laws we usually think of—like the law of gravity or the laws of genetics—there are *natural laws of human behavior* which, if ignored, will produce disastrous results in our lives. Conversely, if we internalize those natural laws of behavior, we can significantly increase our personal productivity and happiness. But only if we understand and live in accordance with them. If we ignore or fight these laws, they will bring pain and unhappiness into our lives, as certainly as defying the law of gravity will bring injury or death. These natural laws have consistent, predictable consequences. They exist whether or not we recognize them. And they exert their effects on us without our consent or awareness.

Now, we can't do much about the world we live in. It is a busy place and is likely to get much busier. The need for ever-increasing personal productivity and the demands on our time will not go away just because we wish they would. But we can do a great deal about *our response to external forces*. We can gain control of our lives to a far greater degree than many of us imagine. The secret lies in understanding and applying certain natural laws.

The natural laws featured in this book are laws that govern personal productivity and fulfillment. The ten that I have chosen are only a few of the natural laws that are available to us. The chapters in Part I focus on five natural laws that will help you better manage your *time*. Part II encompasses five additional natural laws that, when understood and mastered, will give you increased control of your *life*.

Part I: Managing Your Time

Law 1: You control your life by controlling your time.

Law 2: Your governing values are the foundation of personal success and fulfillment.

Law 3: When your daily activities reflect your governing values, you experience inner peace.

Law 4: To reach any significant goal, you must leave your comfort zone.

Law 5: Consistent daily planning leverages time and increases focus.

Part II: Managing Your Life

Law 6: Your behavior is a reflection of what you *truly* believe.

Law 7: You satisfy needs when your beliefs are in line with reality.

Law 8: Negative behaviors are overcome by changing incorrect beliefs.

Law 9: Your self-esteem must ultimately come from within.

Law 10: *Give* more and you'll have more.

These ten natural laws work. I know this from my own experience and from the experiences of thousands of others who have put them to the test. If you apply them, you will find inner peace, perhaps the most desirable gift you can obtain in this life.

PART I

Managing Your Time

"Someday, when I get time, I'm going to . . ." How many times have you said those words or something similar? The desire to get organized, to get the events in our lives under our control, to find time to do things we really want to, is felt by most of us at one time or another. That's why time management is the most commonly taught skill in corporate training, and time management or other "How to Get Organized" seminars are widely attended throughout the United States and in many other countries.

The trouble with most time management instruction is that it focuses only on getting things done more efficiently. No one ever tells you to ask yourself, "Why am I doing this?" or "Should I really be doing this?" or "Do I want to do this?" And unless you are consistently making the opportunity to accomplish things that are important or meaningful to you, being better organized will only fill up your time and make you more frustrated.

As we proceed through the first five natural laws, the ones specifically dealing with managing your time, you'll quickly see that the heart of what I'll be talking about is helping you identify what you really *want* to do, not just the mechanics of keeping track of what you're doing. Unless what you are doing on a daily basis reflects your most deeply held values, you will never experience inner peace.

LAW 1

You control your life
by controlling your time

If I were to stop you on the street and say, "Excuse me, what time is it?" what would you do? You'd probably look at your watch and say, "It's a quarter to three," or some such thing. But if I were to stop you on the street and say the same words but in a different order, *"Time,* what is it?" you'd probably look at me as if I were crazy. In America we don't usually stop people on the street and ask them philosophical questions.

What is time? How would you define it?

Saint Augustine once tried to answer this question. He said: "For what is time? Who is able easily and briefly to explain it? . . . Surely we understand well enough when we speak of it. What then is time? If nobody asks me, I know; but if I were desirous to explain it to someone— plainly I know not." The astute Augustine obviously wasn't much help on this matter.

For centuries, philosophers and wise men have tried to explain time. Sir Isaac Newton said that time was absolute, that it occurred whether the universe was here or not. Leibnitz came along and turned Newton's definition upside down. He said, "Time is merely the order of events, not an entity itself." Albert Einstein followed Leibnitz, and made the

19

statement that "Time has no independent existence apart from the order of events by which we measure it." He then developed an idea called "simultaneous events." He said the train does not arrive at the station at 7:00 P.M.; the train arrives at the station at the same moment the little hand reaches seven.

The definition from the dictionary says: "Time is a continuum in which events succeed one another from past through present to future."

The basic element of time is an event. Everything is an event. Reading this book is an event. Getting out of bed this morning is an event. Driving your car is an event. Arriving at work is an event. Your phone ringing is an event. Eating lunch is an event. Time is the occurrence of all these events in sequence, one after the other.

I was in New York doing a time management seminar for Merrill Lynch executives, when a fellow handed me a card on which he had written his definition of time: "Time is what keeps one darned thing after another from becoming every darned thing at once." Time is a series, or a succession, of events. Ben Franklin said, "Dost thou love life? Then do not squander time, for that's the stuff life is made of." If this is true, then *controlling your life means controlling your time, and controlling your time means controlling the events in your life.*

Gaining Control of Events

Have you ever heard someone say, "I've lost control of my life"? There are times when I look in the mirror and say, "Boy, you're out of control!" What I'm really saying is, "I am no longer in control of the events that make up my life. I am *reacting* to events. I do what everybody else thinks I ought to do, when they think I ought to do it." Being out of control is a terrible feeling.

Think about a rather unusual question that is directly related to the issue of control. *What person has almost absolute total control over the events in his or her professional environment?* I once asked this question to a group of two hundred General Motors employees. One man spoke up and said, "Mothers." There were eighty-three women in the room, and they were ready to stone him.

The answer given by some experts is a symphony conductor. What mental picture do you get of a symphony conductor? Zubin Mehta or someone like him stands up, raises his baton—and what happens? A 110-piece orchestra responds right on cue, and every time that baton moves, the orchestra follows. Wonderful control. Is that the way it is in your life? Wouldn't it be great if we could get that kind of control over the events in our lives?

Now, what group of people has the shortest life expectancy in this country? Probably the members of the orchestra. They live in the reactive world. They spend their lives trying to keep up with the guy with the stick. But the real issue is this: How much control do *we* have?

The diagram below shows what I call the control continuum.

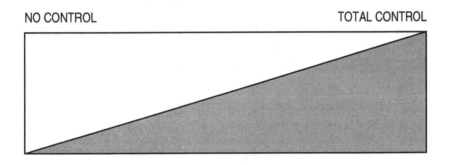

On the right side are events over which you have *total control*. The left side represents events over which you have absolutely *no control*. Everything in between is *partially controlled*. What are some events over which you have no control? The sunrise. Certain illnesses. Tornadoes. Death. Your boss. The stock market. The Super Bowl. You'd be surprised how many things we have absolutely no control over.

What is important is not that there are uncontrollable events in our lives, but how we respond to them. Often the most realistic response is to *adapt*. Live with it. Roll with it. It makes no sense to get upset over things we can't control. Instead, we must adapt. The only other choice is to be perpetually stressed out.

I frequently ask people in our seminars to describe how they feel inside when they face events they can't control. They invariably use words like *frustration, stress, anger*, and *fear*. What level of self-esteem is associated with these words? Obviously, it's low. It doesn't feel good to be out of control.

Perhaps you snow ski. For me, that is an out-of-control experience. I grew up in the Hawaiian Islands and there's not a lot of snow skiing there. In 1982, I moved to Salt Lake City. After living there for three years, my wife and I decided to go skiing, just so we could carry on a decent conversation in our neighborhood. We went to a ski resort at Park City and got in a line for the longest ski lift there. Why? Everybody was getting on this lift. It never occurred to us to get lessons or anything. Halfway up the mountain it dawned on me that the seats on the other side were coming back empty. Now this bothered me, because the lift never stops. I asked my wife, "How do you get off this lift?" I soon found out. You *ski* off the lift. I wish I had a videotape of my first exit from the lift. That was definitely *not* a controlled event. In fact, I experienced all the words I just listed—with one addition, *pain*. Believe me, it doesn't feel good to be out of control.

There are events, however, over which we can have total control. Think about it. What can you control? The list is actually considerable. It includes such things as the time when you get up, what you wear, how you react to somebody else's attitude, what you eat. What do these events all focus on? You. The only thing you have absolute and total control over is *you*. Everything else is partial control or no control.

Make a list of some of the different events in your life. Then assign each event a number from 1 to 5 to indicate the degree of control you have over them, with 5 representing total control and 1 representing no control. Your list might include events like these:

Event	*Degree of Control*
• Time I get out of bed	5
• What I eat	4
• What I wear (to comply with company dress code)	3
• Length of my commute to work	2
• Meeting with my boss	1
• Meeting with a subordinate	4
• Lunchtime and with whom	3
• How I react to a colleague I don't care for	5
• Traffic on way home	1
• What I do this evening	5
• What I do tomorrow night	1

Your list may be entirely different, but make note of some of the typical events you encounter in life. Then study the list and ask, "How much control do I have over my life?" Even if there seem to be relatively few things you control, the skills and tools presented in this book will help you exercise greater control than you presently do.

Now, what words describe how you feel when you control the events that you are able to control? You may feel *confident, happy, exhilarated, powerful*, maybe even *surprised*. But there are two words that encompass all the feelings we get when we *are* in control: *inner peace*. What is inner peace? *Inner peace is having serenity, balance, and harmony in our lives through the appropriate control of events.*

So, the objective of good time management is inner peace. But before we go further, you need to stop thinking "time management" and start thinking "event control." Too often we think time management has something to do with our watch. The only thing a watch tells you is how long it takes the sun to go across the sky. That's an event over which we have no control. The real issue is: What *events* can *I* control? Focusing on "event control" makes all the difference.

Conditioning

Part of the reason some of us fail to take control lies in our individual conditioning. Many of us have been conditioned to accept less than we can have and be less than we can be. That point is well made by a story I heard from my partner, Dick Winwood, who once took his daughter, Sarah, to a traveling circus. Dick was surprised to find eight elephants, each tethered only by a small rope attached to a ring on an iron leg shackle. Each of the small ropes, in turn, was tied to a much larger rope that was staked to the ground. Any one of those elephants, as big and strong as each was, could easily have walked away to explore the shopping mall across the highway. Dick wondered why these intelligent and curious creatures would not *want* to be free and roam around.

Later, he did some research to learn why elephants stay tethered when they have the power to move about. He learned that when they are very young, those elephants are chained by the leg to immovable stakes. For several weeks they struggle to free themselves. But, little by little, over a period of three or four weeks, the elephants are conditioned to believe that they can't move about freely when they are tied by the right rear leg. From the moment this conditioning takes hold, you can tie them with a string and they won't move. The elephants at the circus didn't roam about because they *believed* they couldn't. The tethers *in their minds* were stronger than any chain or rope.

Now, we're not elephants. But in many subtle ways we've been conditioned to believe certain things about ourselves and our environment. And we need to erase two effects of this conditioning from our lives if we want control and inner peace. These two effects are illustrated by the following statements:

There are events we can't control, but we believe we can. We waste time complaining about the weather, or futilely trying to control or manipulate spouses or employees or our children.

Conversely, *there are events we can control, but we believe we can't.* Many people, for example, feel that they are locked into careers they really don't like, but in reality this is usually self-imposed bondage.

Some events *are* literally beyond our capacity to control, but for some reason we get it in our heads that we *can* control them. When I asked in a recent seminar for an example of something we can't control, one man in the audience said, "My wife." True. Usually, you can't control other people or what they do. If you try to control them, you'll probably end up in jail. You can influence their behavior; but you can't control them.

What about children? We may think that they are under our control during their growing years, because as babies they start out being under almost our total control when they're born. At that time we can't control some things about them, but they are almost totally dependent on us and we can control a great deal. With every passing day, though, they march (or crawl) a little further toward the "no control" side of the model. When they become teenagers they seem to *leap* toward that side of the model. Let us hope that by the time they are young adults, they are relatively independent of our control. We succeed as parents to the degree that we help this transfer of control from parent to child take place.

If, in the long run, we can't control even our own children, can we realistically expect to control other people not so intimately connected with us? We may think we can and we may impact their behavior to some degree, but ultimately *what other people do is out of our control.*

By contrast, there are some events we really can control, but mentally and emotionally we believe we can't. Suppose, for example, that you are in your hotel room at the Marriott Marquis in Manhattan and I call you from JFK Airport. I say, "Listen, if you meet me at the Delta terminal at four-thirty, I'll give you a check for five hundred thousand dollars." You look at your watch, and it's quarter to four. You have forty-five minutes to get there. Your first thought is, No way. With the detours and daytime traffic, it took me an hour and a half to get here in a taxi from JFK. You might just assume you have no control over the situation—there's no way you can get that $500,000. But wait a minute. We're talking about half a million dollars! Half a million dollars can give you options you normally wouldn't have. You get on the phone and call the Marquis operator. "Has this hotel got a helicopter pad?" you ask. "No," the operator informs you, "but there's one eleven blocks away at the Pan Am Building." "Great!" you say. "Now, listen carefully. I've got a thousand dollars for you if you get the helicopter service on the line double-quick." The operator earns her thousand dollars, and you tell the startled voice on the phone, "Look, if you'll bump all your other passengers and get me to JFK Airport in the next half hour, I'll give you fifty thousand dollars." After checking with management, the voice says, "How soon can you get here?" One way or another, we'd very likely be at the Delta terminal before the appointed hour. The point here is that when the need is big enough, we control all kinds of events that we normally believe we can't control. The only difference is our *need* to control them.

I grew up in Honolulu, and when I was eleven years old I decided I could swim across Hanauma Bay, on the southern tip of Oahu. It's a beautiful place, a mile and a quarter across, with water about eighty feet deep. I went there, dove into the water, and started to swim across. Well, the waves were quite big that day, and I couldn't see the other side. Halfway across, I started to drown. You get some interesting feelings when you think you're going to drown. I was treading water, facing out to sea, when all of a sudden I saw a fin gliding through the water about ten feet away. My need to get to the other side went absolutely crazy. What I discovered about myself was this: It's okay to drown. It's *not* okay to get eaten. I make a big issue of this control thing because it *is* a big issue. We talk ourselves into believing we cannot control events that we really can control. We give up when our options are by no means exhausted.

The Productivity Tri-quation

Psychologist Nathaniel L. Branden, author of *The Psychology of Self-Esteem*, once pointed out the direct relationship between self-esteem and productive work. In essence, Branden observed that the better you feel about yourself, the more productive you will be; and the more productive you are, the better you will feel about yourself. I like Branden's observation, but it doesn't go far enough for me. If we add a third element to this equation, event control, it becomes what we might call a "tri-quation." The productivity tri-quation is shown below.

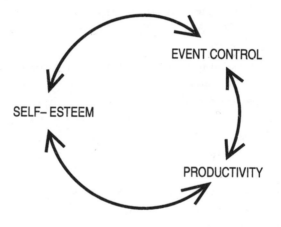

Remember your eighth-grade algebra for a moment. When you take something from the left side of an equation, what do you have to take from the right side to keep it equal? The same amount. What that means in terms of our tri-quation is this: If my self-esteem drops, what tends to happen to my productivity? It drops too. And if my productivity drops, so does my event control. The antithesis of this is also true: Higher self-esteem raises productivity *and* event control. The easiest part of this tri-quation to attack is the event control piece. If I can exert greater control over the events in my life, I can become more productive, better organized, and spend more time on activities that are of value to me. The natural by-product of that is an increase in my sense of self-worth.

Now, I'm not suggesting that we don't have intrinsic value in and of ourselves, because we do. What I am suggesting is that as I get more control over the events in my life, I feel better about myself. And as I get more control over things that matter a great deal to me, I feel terrific. Keeping in mind that we want to control those events that matter most to us, consider the following questions:

1. What are the highest priorities in your life?
2. Of these priorities, which do you value the most?

In the next several chapters, we will deal with the process of identifying and giving precedence to the highest priorities in our lives—those things that matter most to us and that are essential for us to be doing something about if we are to experience true inner peace.

Not only are the answers to these two questions important, but what we *do* with the answers is also important. The first question is about identifying our inner core values, the things that are most important to us—something we'll talk more about in the next chapter. The second question suggests some kind of sequencing, because some priorities and events are obviously more important than others. Once we've identified the events that matter most, the issue then becomes: How do we act on them? How do we get control of the most crucial events?

Two Time Fallacies

We've already established that controlling our lives means controlling our time, and that controlling our time means controlling the events in our lives. Why, then, do most of us have so much trouble accomplishing the things that mean the most to us in the long term? Why do we never seem to get around to those things that really matter? There are several possible answers to this dilemma. One is that we've unwittingly bought into two fallacies about time that prevent us from dealing effectively with the events in our lives.

The first fallacy is that we think *we're going to have more time at some unspecified future date than we do now.* "Well, I'll do that next week, or next month, or next year, or when the children are grown, or when I retire. Then I'll have more time." The second fallacy is that we think *we can somehow save time.* The fact is, you *have* all the time there is. You're given a check every day for twenty-four hours, and you have to spend every last second. You get 86,400 seconds each day, no more, no less, and you can't save any of them to spend at a later date. That means, when you say to someone, "I don't have time," you are not telling the truth. You have as much time as anyone else.

If you called me on the phone today and said, "Hyrum, I'd like you to have dinner with me tonight," and I answered, "Sorry, I would really like to have dinner with you tonight, but I just don't have time," I would be lying. What I am really saying is: "I value some other event more than having dinner with you." Why don't I just come out and say that? Well, it's culturally okay to say, "I don't have time." It is *not* culturally okay to say, "I value another event more than having dinner with you—so I'm not going!" That would be an insult.

Usually, we don't even understand what we're saying when we tell people we don't have time to do something. And they don't understand either. That's why they're usually not offended. But how often do we tell *ourselves* subtle lies to convince ourselves we don't have time to do something? How often do we leave important matters undone because we think we "don't have time"? What we're really saying is that we've allowed insignificant events, like watching TV or doing a crossword puzzle, to become more valuable to us than significant events, like playing with our children or getting to know our neighbors better or writing the book we've always intended to write.

In the next chapter we'll talk specifically about values and priorities and how to identify those things that matter most. For now, though, we just need to recognize that we don't always do those things that are most important to us. We have a limited supply of time, and somehow it seems to slip away from us, almost as if someone is stealing it.

Time Robbers

Have you ever noticed that the things that matter most often get pushed aside by less important concerns? Everyone and everything, at times, seem to conspire against us and prevent us from accomplishing what we really want to. Events we never anticipated catch us blind side, demand our attention, and distract us from what matters most. These events control us, and when that happens, our productivity drops and so does our self-esteem. Because these events deflect us from what we really ought to be doing, they are very costly.

Do you know what opportunity cost is? Suppose I give you ten thousand dollars in hundred-dollar bills and instruct you to spend the money before midnight. That's it. At midnight I'm going to show up at your door and take back any money you haven't spent. You lose it. Would you have any money left at midnight? Of course not. Now, what you spend it on is your business, but let's say you spend the money on clothes. By making that decision, what have you decided *not* to spend the money on? Everything else. So the opportunity cost of the clothes is what else you could have spent the money on.

Time is just like money. When you decide to spend one hour watching TV, you have also decided not to spend the time on what? Everything else.

You would be very upset if someone gained access to your bank account and stole all your money. Most people, though, don't blink an eye when all sorts of culprits sneak into their lives and steal their time.

The list of "time robbers" below is not exhaustive, but perhaps it will help put you on guard against influences that can steal your most precious commodity, time. I've divided these time robbers into two groups for a reason. Group A time robbers are usually imposed by the environment where you work. Those in Group B are most often self-inflicted.

TIME ROBBERS

Group A: Imposed on Us	*Group B: Self-inflicted*
_____ Interruptions	_____ Failure to delegate
_____ Waiting for answers	_____ Poor attitude
_____ Unclear job definition	_____ Personal disorganization
_____ Unnecessary meetings	_____ Absentmindedness
_____ Too much work	_____ Failure to listen
_____ Poor communication	_____ Indecision
_____ Shifting priorities	_____ Socializing
_____ Equipment failure	_____ Fatigue
_____ Disorganized boss	_____ Lack of self-discipline
_____ Red tape	_____ Leaving tasks unfinished
_____ Conflicting priorities	_____ Paper shuffling

_____ Low company morale _____ Procrastination
_____ Untrained staff _____ Outside activities
_____ Peer/staff demands _____ Cluttered workspace
_____ Lack of authority _____ Unclear personal goals
_____ Interoffice travel _____ Perfectionism
_____ Mistakes of others _____ Poor planning
_____ Revised deadlines _____ Preoccupation
_____ Meetings _____ Attempting too much

Not all of these time robbers are avoidable. Some, like meetings and lack of authority, may be beyond our control. But most of them simply creep into our lives and steal from us without our ever being aware of them. Suddenly our time is gone, we've spent our daily allotment, and we don't know where it went. We might say that the opportunity cost of these time robbers is very high—especially in terms of event control, personal productivity, and self-esteem.

As you read through the list, identify the time robbers that give you the greatest difficulty. Give them a ranking, from one to ten, and then carefully consider how you might eliminate the worst ten pickpockets.

In case you're wondering how your list compares to others, we ask our seminar participants to identify their biggest time robbers. The participants represent a very diverse group of people and professions, and the five most popular time robbers are:

1. Interruptions
2. Procrastination
3. Shifting priorities
4. Poor planning
5. Waiting for answers

Three of this infamous five came from the "A" list of time robbers imposed on us by others, and two came from the "B" list of self-inflicted time robbers. But the sad thing about all five of these time robbers is that they are habitual behaviors with most of us. In other words, the ways you wasted time today are much the same as the ways you wasted time last week and last month. And *unless you identify the principal culprits and create a plan for eliminating them, you will continue wasting time in the same pattern every day for the rest of your life.* With this in mind, let me offer a few suggestions for obliterating these common time robbers.

Interruptions

Unwanted telephone calls and drop-in visitors cut into high-priority tasks like a meat cleaver. While we outwardly endure interruptions, we most often inwardly resent the intrusion on our time.

When asked to suggest ways of handling interruptions, most people produce a long list of tactics designed to ward off, ignore, or cut short any infringement on their time. They assume that handling interruptions is the same as getting rid of people. But while some interruptions are unnecessary and unwarranted, even annoying, others are very necessary. For most of us, if we didn't have an interruption for two straight days, we wouldn't have a job. The real question is: "How can I tell a high-priority interruption from a dysfunctional interruption?" Interruptions generally fall under one of three categories:

1. *Unnecessary interruptions* occur when someone drops in unannounced or calls on the phone, mistakenly assuming that you care, that you have the required information, or that you are responsible. If none of these is true, then this is an unnecessary intrusion—a waste of time. This interruption is to be avoided or terminated quickly.
2. *Necessary interruptions* are those about which you *do* care, for which you have information or responsibility. A necessary interruption has value, and you should handle it at once—unless it is untimely.
3. *Untimely interruptions* are necessary, but come at an inconvenient or inappropriate time. These should be rescheduled to a more suitable time.

An effective tool for determining quickly the type of an interruption is the "point question." The point question is simply a nonthreatening query designed to get to the point of the interruption: "Carol, nice to see you. How can I help you today?" "What brings you around today?" "What can I do for you?"

When a person interrupts you, they never begin by telling you what type of interruption they are. So you ask the point question to find out. In essence, you are transferring "ownership" of the conversation to the interrupting person. The subtle, underlying message is for them to quickly justify their intrusion. They respond with a need or question, you instantly evaluate the priority and the time necessary to respond to the question or need, then act accordingly. Let me illustrate.

Janet is sitting at her desk involved in an urgent and important task that will take up the remainder of the afternoon. Suddenly the phone rings. She answers it, and on the other end is a co-worker from another department.

"Janet, this is Tom. How are you doing?"

"Fine, Tom. What can I do for you?"

"Well, at lunch last week you said you wanted to get together to discuss a proposal for coordinating activities between our departments. I've got an hour or so right now. I thought it might be a good time for you."

"Tom, we definitely need to meet, but at the moment I'm up against an important deadline. Can we make it tomorrow at two?"

"I think I'm free at two. Let's make it tomorrow, then."

"Fine. See you then."

Notice that this conversation started with a comment that could have led practically anywhere. Janet's question got Tom to the point, and Janet was then able to determine what type of interruption it was (untimely) and respond accordingly (reschedule).

Many interruptions can be avoided by scheduling a regular one-on-one meeting with people who frequently come to you with concerns or questions. By doing this, you can prevent them from interrupting you unless it's an urgent, high-priority matter, in other words, a necessary interruption.

Interruptions are not all bad, of course. Sometimes the interruption is more important than whatever it is you've been working on. Sometimes opportunity knocks unannounced and at untimely moments. If you are in control of how you handle interruptions and, consequently, view them in a positive light, you will be better prepared to seize these opportunities and put them to work for you.

Procrastination

Whereas interruptions are the most common form of "other-inflicted" time robber, procrastination is the most common (and most readily admitted) self-inflicted time robber. To some, procrastination is a casual visitor, here today, gone tomorrow; to others it is a nagging mother-in-law, who comes for a weekend visit but ends up moving in.

At the Franklin Quest Company, we have identified two basic varieties of procrastination:

> *Conscious*—where we are "awake" and aware of what we are doing, and
> *Unconscious*—where we are almost totally unaware of our actions.

Conscious procrastination is easiest to identify and offer specific responses to. Unconscious procrastination is a bit more difficult—because we must "catch" ourselves doing it. Either way, procrastination carries a high opportunity cost. "Putting it off" has probably caused more heartache and failure than all other time management problems combined. Opportunity knocks just as often at the procrastinator's door as at anyone else's. But the procrastinator doesn't answer.

Why do we procrastinate? In other words, why do we often allow the things that matter most to be at the mercy of things that matter least? Perhaps the most common reason is that certain important tasks are unpleasant. Some people absolutely hate balancing their checkbook, for instance, or filling out monthly reports, or doing their taxes, or meeting new people, or speaking before groups, or answering their mail, or taking out the garbage, or going to the dentist, or exercising. Being productive and successful and healthy often requires us to leave our comfort zones. The natural response to unpleasant tasks is to put them off. But if we put them off, we let events control us, our productivity drops, and so does our self-esteem. The only way to escape this downward spiral is to exert control over the events in our lives, even if some of them are unpleasant.

Here are some suggestions for overcoming procrastination:

- *Set a deadline*, which creates an urgency where before there was none.

- *Do the most unpleasant part first.* By doing this, you can look forward to the more enjoyable tasks and end your day with a positive feeling.
- *Make a game of it.* This is an effective way of turning drudgery into fun.
- *Build in a reward*, which gives you incentive to complete the task quickly.

Another reason we procrastinate is because some tasks seem overwhelming to us, because of their size, duration, or complexity. Quick, easy, fun tasks are always more enjoyable, but we can make monstrous tasks less overwhelming if we take Henry Ford's advice: "Nothing is particularly hard if you divide it into small jobs."

Other reasons for procrastinating important tasks include: overcommitting (which has a paralyzing effect), lack of information, unclear goals, fear of failure, poor timing, and general disorganization. Or, we may procrastinate a task because of apathy—we really don't care whether it gets done or not. If we are aware of the reasons for our procrastination, we can attack the problem more directly. Regardless of the reason, procrastination is a deadly time robber—and the best way of overcoming it is to somehow infuse the procrastinated task with a sense of urgency.

Shifting Priorities

Here's a time robber that creates more confusion in the workplace than any other. Working in such a place might be better described as belonging to the "Crisis of the Week Club." Shifting priorities commonly identify a work environment where things are moving very fast. Management, in an effort to respond quickly to problems or opportunities, shifts the energies of the organization from one "battlefront" to another as the situation warrants. This can be very exciting and a real rush for some personalities, but only if the shifts and starts have meaning and purpose. Without seeing purpose, people will feel as if they're getting jerked around. This especially happens when the "Crisis of the Week (or day, month, etc.)" doesn't get solved, and people just move on to a new crisis.

The effect of shifting priorities has actually been examined in scientific experiments. Scientists have conducted studies where rats are conditioned to certain noises, smells, and procedures which will bring the rats a desired food. Once the rats learn the procedures involved, they can gain access to this food whenever they want. The result is extremely healthy and happy rats. Once the rats have reached this happy state, however, the scientists begin to change the rule (shift the priorities). Now, the rats find that following the usual procedures does not produce the desired results. When they learn the new procedure, the rules are changed again and the rats have to start over from scratch. After experiencing several of these shifts in direction, the rats at first respond by being irritable and nasty with each other. Then, reaching a level of maximum frustration, they either sit and do nothing or even die.

We're not rats, nor are our work environments manipulated in such an extreme manner. There are some interesting parallels, however. If you are reaching the point of frustration with such priority shifts, I suggest that you consult with your manager. What you're seeking here is understanding and how you can best adapt to the situation and be productive. The alternatives are simple, really. You can flee (take off, find a new job, sit and do nothing, even die) or flow (learn to move with the current and enjoy the trip). Remember our discussion of the control continuum of events we totally control, events we can't control at all, and everything in between. A workplace with shifting priorities is a situation where you probably have very little control, and the only workable response is to flow or adapt.

Poor Planning

It's an old axiom that "If you fail to plan, you plan to fail." Poor planning is an obviously self-imposed time robber and on the surface appears to have an equally obvious solution—*superior* planning! Yet, the symptoms of poor plans typically derive from the environment you work in or from a lack of understanding about the benefits of control via planning.

For example, if there is an unending press of work—each task screaming for your attention—the result can be an attitude of "What difference does it make where I start?" Also, if the work environment is highly distracting due to any number of reasons, trying to formulate a plan can be frustrating. The feeling often can be, "It's not worth it. I'll just get on with my job."

Neither situation is very fulfilling and neither is justifiable if you really want to exercise a measure of control and have a claim to inner peace.

That's why I spend so much time in my seminars and in this book hammering on the process of planning and prioritizing, and the importance of discipline in both planning and following through to implement your plans. If you recognize poor planning as one of the major time robbers for you, I strongly suggest that you pay special attention to Law 4 and Law 5 in this book.

Waiting for Answers

"Good things come to those who wait." Somebody once said that. It wasn't me. I hate to wait. Yet, waiting for answers is a commonly identified time robber—everyone is impacted by this one from time to time. It's environmentally imposed—meaning you lack a measure of control. So, adapting or flowing is a necessary response most of the time.

However, in waiting for someone else to provide answers, I have found that we often have more control than we realize but fail to use it. If organizational priorities have identified my task as vital, I need to do whatever I can to break the "log jam" to get the answers (or information, or product, or equipment, etc.) that I need. Here are some tactics that have worked for me:

1. Call the person you are waiting on and explain your priority and the problem. Ask for special help or at least a place or person you can go to for help.
2. Follow up on all leads, and at each point stress need and desired result. Ask what you can do to help the situation.
3. If you run into a higher management level than you're at, enlist the help of your manager. Elevate the problem until either the problem is solved or you reach an unavoidable blockage.
4. Make sure all involved know to contact you as soon as possible when the answer, information, etc., is available.

If you find that literally nothing can be done, then move on with your next most pressing problem or task. It's time to flow.

Having given a more definitive treatise on the five major time robbers, allow me to make a quick statement on each of the other time robbers.

These surfaced as significant problems for many executives all over the world.

First, let's consider Group A, the time robbers that are imposed on us:

Unclear job definition: In this situation, we just don't know what we are expected to do. It's like speeding down a highway and running into a bank of fog. You slow down and move slowly. Why? Because you can't see. When the fog dissipates and clears up, you move faster. What is the only thing that changed? The clarity of the picture. At work, when you don't know where you are or where you are going, your productivity drops. Whose responsibility is it to clearly define your job? If you haven't been able to do it yourself, then the obligation is on you to sit down with your supervisor and identify a clear picture of your responsibilities. Until that is done, tremendous amounts of time will be wasted.

Unnecessary meetings: In America it is estimated that over eleven million meetings are held each day. Many of these are too long and many are not even necessary. How do we fix that? If you're calling the meeting, be sure to identify an objective for the meeting, create an agenda, and make sure only the appropriate people are in attendance. If someone is there who does not need to be there, excuse that person so he/she can get on with more productive things. If you're supposed to attend someone else's meeting and you question the need for you to be there, check to see how necessary your attendance is and maybe you can be excused.

Too much work: This is another name for overload. Remember that we all have Plimsoll lines. In 1880, Samuel Plimsoll of the United Kingdom tackled the problem of having overloaded ships sink in heavy seas. He submitted a bill in Parliament insisting that a line be drawn around the outside of the hull on all British ships. When the ships were loaded with freight and reached the level where the line hit the water, the ships were not allowed to load any more freight. That marking on a ship's hull became known as the Plimsoll line. Human beings have Plimsoll lines, and although they are invisible, they are drawn right under the nose. Some days, all we can say is "Don't make a ripple." And there are times when we just have to say no. If you are planning your day appropriately, you will have the necessary ammunition to say no. The task can then be reassigned or some of the tasks you have can be reevaluated in order for you to make available time for the urgent tasks. Learn to say no.

Poor communication: Untold hours, days, weeks, even years are lost when we do not communicate well. Often this goes back to having a clear picture in your mind. If you have a clear picture of what is expected and you can communicate that to others who are going to be participating in the completion of the task, tremendous amounts of time will be saved. If you are unable to transfer to others a clear picture of what is expected, then much time will be wasted.

Equipment failure: What can I say? Has anyone ever waited for a computer that has gone down? There are two major issues here. 1.) Preventive maintenance. Try to make sure it does not go down in the first place. And 2.) Have a standard operating procedure to fix down equipment or at least to have a backup available immediately so that time is not lost by equipment failure. Millions of dollars are lost each year because of equipment downtime. Fix it!

Disorganized boss: For someone who is naturally organized, to have to work for a supervisor who is unorganized is extremely discouraging. Once again, communication in this situation is the key. Make sure your supervisor understands what you are doing, expectations for your productivity are agreed upon, and times are agreed upon. Over time, this will tend to encourage the supervisor to be organized as well.

Red tape: As companies grow and bureaucracies flourish, the issue of red tape tends to become a real problem. How do we get around that? 1.) Understand the fact that it exists, and 2.) Be proactive enough not to allow the red tape issue to get in your way. If you know there is red tape, then plan around it. There is always a solution to getting through red tape.

Conflicting priorities: When agreement has not been reached between a supervisor and an employee as to a priority of a given set of tasks, we always have a major problem. Make sure that the priorities are agreed upon and then work hard to make sure those priorities are met.

Low company morale: Low morale often comes from a lack of self-esteem, not knowing what is expected, commitments and promises not being kept by individuals and organizations. There are many causes for this one. The fix is to ensure that everyone has daily victories. The organization needs it. Each individual in the organization needs it. How to do it? Do what you have to do to increase the productivity. See that the victories occur every single day.

Untrained staff: If you're the boss, train them. If you're the one that needs training, get it.

Peer/staff demands: This is another time robber where the answer lies in developing the ability to say no. If you have planned your day properly, you will have a pretty good feel for what you can accomplish today. As extraneous demands come from peers and staff members, let them know that what they are asking does not fit. If it is a crisis, then you can have a collective decision to override what you have chosen to do for the day. That will rarely happen if you have planned properly.

Lack of authority: This is a frustrating challenge for managers and executives all over the world. The problem often comes back to poor communication. When you are accepting a responsibility, make sure you have a clear vision and understanding with your supervisor about exactly what your authority will be for completing the task. To launch into a task that you think you have the authority to accomplish and then discover that you don't is extremely frustrating and stressful. Get agreement up front so there are no surprises about what your authority is.

Interoffice travel: There seems to be a group of people in every organization who seem to take great pleasure in floating from office to office to see what is going on, to visit, to get the latest gossip. Go back to my discussion on interruptions and just don't let this occur.

Mistakes of others: These are going to happen. We have to work around them; be patient with them. Insist that mistakes are openly communicated in a positive, constructive way. Over time, they will begin to shrink.

Revised deadlines: Depending where you are in the organization there may not be a lot you can do with this one. If you have no say on deadlines, you may have to be totally flexible. If you have input, make sure you give it.

Now, some thoughts about Group B, the self-inflicted time robbers:

Failure to delegate: This one touches a raw nerve. When you get into an automobile full of people, whom do you prefer to drive the car? If you're like most people, it is generally *yourself*. Why? Because, in your view, no one else drives a car better than you do or is safer than you when driving. That tends to be the attitude we bring into everything we do. "I have to do it myself or it won't be done well." In fact, a major reduction in stress will be experienced when you are willing to admit that someone else can do it just as well as you can and perhaps, God forbid, even better. Delegate it!

Poor attitude: Poor attitudes can be fatal. They will always slow down your productivity. How do we change our attitudes about ourselves? Generally, in my experience, communication is the key. Quite often people do not even know they are exhibiting a poor attitude. If you have the poor attitude yourself, I hope the people around you will have the courage to let you know that you are part of the problem, not part of the solution. In Part II of this book, I'll talk more about how we acquire the beliefs we have about ourselves, how they affect our behavior, and how to change those beliefs and their resulting attitudes.

Personal disorganization: If it takes you twice as long to do something as it does someone else, that should be a message to you. This entire book is about increasing our ability to be organized. If there is one key here it is daily planning. Identifying what matters, putting it in some sort of order that makes sense, and then following your plan.

Absentmindedness: Everyone, to a degree, has brushes with absentmindedness. In chapter 5 I will describe a time management tool that will make it pretty hard for anything to slip through the cracks. Don't rely on your ability to remember an event, a time, or an agreement. Write it down, have a follow-up system which is impeccable, and this problem will go away.

Failure to listen: Books have been written about the skill of listening. To fix this one in a sentence is absurd. However, be assured that sharpening your ability to listen will hasten communication and understanding and save enormous amounts of time as well.

Indecision: Indecision often is a result of not having enough information about the task or problem you are trying to solve. Sometimes indecision occurs because it is risky to make decisions and we do not like to fail. Get all the information you possibly can, weigh the relative merits, and make the best decision possible. When no decision is made, we too often find that it is made for us by circumstances or by other people, with results that may or may not be beneficial for us. The productive person learns that an occasional mistake is preferable to the paralysis of indecision.

Socializing: I once received a letter from an executive in California who discovered from a self-administered time log that he was socializing on the job a total of nine hours per week. That is a full day's work. I'm not suggesting that all socializing is bad because quite often good information is transferred in the socializing process. Just be aware of the fact, however, that many hours per week can be lost in unproductive visiting. The coffeepot crowd can be a lethal group in all organizations.

Fatigue: During my years in sales management, I would tell my salespeople that their physical well-being had a major impact on how much they could sell. Many of them did not believe that. Those that did discovered the magic of being in good shape, getting enough sleep, and eating properly. Fatigue is very flagging and will bring productivity down every time.

Lack of self-discipline: I have a colleague who has a plaque on his desk that says DO IT, DO IT RIGHT, DO IT RIGHT NOW. We need daily victories. When we accomplish what we have asked ourselves to do each day, what it does for our self-worth is powerful. When we don't do what we ask ourselves to accomplish, it has the opposite effect on self-esteem and just about every other aspect of our lives. Just get it done.

Leaving tasks unfinished: Usually a result of an inability to prioritize or recognize the relative value of a task, this is a time robber that needs to be fixed. If you are properly using the concepts and processes taught in this book, this will not be a problem. A time management tool like the Franklin Day Planner is wonderful for making sure tasks don't fall through the cracks. It will also help you with delegation and making sure that people who work with and for you don't leave tasks unfinished either.

Paper shuffling: Prioritize your paper just like you prioritize your tasks. Have vital, important, and trivial stacks. I even have in my credenza next to my desk three different drawers for A, B, and C paper. Instruct your staff to break the paper down for you. A good secretary will be able to do this in a heartbeat. Deal with the A stuff first. If you have time, then touch the B and C items. Don't touch it unless you have to. Quite often you will discover that your C drawer gets emptied out without you even looking at it.

Outside activities: Everyone should have interests and involvements outside our vocation. In addition to hobbies or similar interests, it's good to be involved in opportunities that help make our community, state, and nation a better place to live. However, we must draw a line that will ensure that these activities do not consume our thinking and production time to a point where it is a detriment to our work (of course, if you're retired or have income that you don't have to work to receive, you can spend as much time as you want in "outside" activities). The solution to spending more time than is appropriate on outside activities is again found in ordering and prioritizing the tasks and events of the day. How much can I accomplish in a day and of those events and tasks are they the most important?

Cluttered workspace: Each of us will have varying ideas about how clear a desk or workspace should be, and to some extent it is a matter of personal preference. But if we can't quickly lay our hands on important papers or information, our productivity is impacted negatively. My friend Dick Winwood suggests organizing your workspace so that those materials of greatest importance and frequency of use are closest to you, while things of lesser value are farther away. Expanding on the thoughts I expressed earlier about how to avoid paper shuffling, remove all unorganized papers from your desktop, desk drawers, "in" and "hold" baskets, and stack them all on the desk directly in front of you. As you go through your stack of paper, ask, "Is this an A (crucial), B (important), or C (low value) or D (no value) item?" Put the A, B, and C items in stacks with others in the same category. The D items can go in the wastebasket. Put the C stack in a bottom drawer of your desk or a credenza. The B's could go into a file folder marked "Important" and placed where it can be easily reached. The A's—your most critical task materials—can go into a file folder marked "Critical" and sit on your desk in a place offering easy access and availability. Another hint: Don't have your "In" basket on your desk, where you'll be tempted to keep looking in it. Instead, put it on a filing cabinet or table where new items can be easily added, but where it won't distract you until you decide to go through it. Just remember that the war on clutter is an ongoing one that will require attention on a regular basis if you are to win.

Unclear personal goals: In the remaining chapters of this section of the book, you will learn how to develop your own personal Productivity Pyramid. Until you take the time to do your productivity pyramid, you may have no idea where you are going, why, or how to get there. Make sure you learn the concepts contained in this book and do your own productivity pyramid, and you will see the power it can have.

Perfectionism: The phrase "paralyzing perfectionism" describes a fascinating concept that can kill productivity. Many of us feel that we have to have everything so perfect that we never start the job in the first place. Some people even have to be sure the stars are just right in the heavens. If you have a job to do, get started on it and do the best you can. Then get on to the next task.

Preoccupation: Daydreaming can be a real time robber. We have time for daydreaming when we lack focus. When we have not planned our day and don't have a good feel for what we are going to do with our hours and minutes, it is easy to sit and daydream. Very little is accomplished in daydreaming unless you have deliberately planned to set thirty minutes or an hour aside, put your feet up on your desk, and think. There are times when this is the most effective thing you can do in a day. That, however, is not daydreaming—it is creative thinking and planning.

Attempting too much: This is the hero syndrome that some of us get trapped into by thinking we can do more than we actually can. To avoid it, we must go back to our planning. Create solid monthly, weekly, and daily plans. If you have built your productivity pyramid properly, prioritized everything properly, you will find yourself being much more realistic about what you can accomplish in a given day.

Many of the natural laws, concepts, and processes presented in this book will help you eliminate or control all of these time robbers. But I hope the ideas I've presented in these few pages will help you realize that you have more control over many time robbers than you may think you have.

"Urgent" Does Not Mean "Vital"

We need to draw a very important distinction between a *vital* and an *urgent* task. An urgent task is something that demands immediate attention. It comes out of left field and says, "Hey, I need to be done right now." What's an example of something that's urgent? By far the most common is the telephone. Every time your phone rings, what is it saying to you? "Pick me up, pick me up, pick me up." You don't go around indiscriminately picking up phones unless they're ringing. And the only thing the ring says is, "I want to be dealt with right now." But are most phone calls important? One or two a day, perhaps, but not the majority of them. Would you like to feel some real power today? Let the phone ring.

Urgencies are not priorities; they act on priorities. For example, suppose we're at the university. You're a student, I'm your professor, and this is the first day of the semester. I hold up a book and say, "Listen, if you want a good grade in my class you'd better become familiar with this book. Why? Because the entire final exam is taken from this book." Now, being a typical college student, do you go out and buy that book and begin devouring it tonight? Not if you're typical. When does that book become urgent? The night before the test. Now, that book has had great value all semester, but until an urgency is placed on it, it tends to lie there.

Let me ask you two revealing questions. First, how many minutes a week does the average father spend with his children in one-on-one conversation? According to a study done a few years ago, the number is seven minutes—seven minutes in an entire week! Is it vital that we spend time with our children, one-on-one? I think everyone would agree it's vital; it has great value. But is it urgent? No. Why not? Because the child is always there. We can do it anytime we want. So we tend to put off the highly valued task because we're dealing with urgencies all day.

Second, how many minutes a week do the average husband and wife spend in one-on-one conversation? According to the study, the number is twenty-seven minutes. Is it vital to spend time with your spouse? I think we'd agree, it's vital. But is it urgent? No. Why not? Same problem—the spouse is always there.

Now, the nice thing about urgencies is that you don't have to worry about them. They surface all by themselves. I was doing a seminar at Citibank in New York several years ago, and I decided to ask this question: "How many of you would like to do more reading?" Every hand in the room went up. "Well," I said, "you've obviously placed a value on reading, but you're not doing it. Why aren't you doing it?" Nobody dared say they didn't have time, right? We'd already blown that excuse away, so it just got stone quiet. Finally, a guy in the last row raised his hand and said, "Books don't ring." What a wonderful response that was! Books don't hop up and say, "Hey, I'm a really great book, why don't you read me?" They just kind of lie there. And until we apply urgency to them, nothing happens.

You need to understand that there's a big difference between important tasks and urgencies. Some tasks are never going to be urgent, even though they may be extremely vital. Other tasks may never be important, but they will be urgent. The secret is to identify your vital activities and infuse them with a sense of urgency, so that they can compete with the activities that have a natural sense of urgency built into them. But how do you make something urgent that has no intrinsic urgency about it? (How do you make a book ring?) The only way to do this is to set up a system that takes your deepest values and translates them into daily activities. As we discussed in this chapter, control of your time goes much deeper than your appointment book. Before you start planning your time you must identify those things that really are the most important in your life. That's what we'll focus on in Law 2—the next chapter.

LAW 2

Your governing values are the foundation of personal fulfillment

When Benjamin Franklin was twenty-two years old—he was living in Philadelphia at the time, having run away from an oppressive apprenticeship in his native Boston—he conceived the "bold and arduous project of arriving at moral perfection." In essence, he asked himself the question: "What are the highest priorities in my life?" From this period of introspection, he emerged with twelve "virtues"—his governing values. So there would be no question in his mind what those values meant to him, he qualified every one of them with a written statement. The result of this exercise is shown below:

Temperance   "Eat not to dullness; drink not to elevation."

Silence   "Speak not but what may benefit others or yourself; avoid trifling conversation."

Order   "Let all your things have their places; let each part of your business have its time."

Resolution   "Resolve to perform what you ought; perform without fail what you resolve."

Frugality	"Make no expense but to do good to others or yourself; that is, waste nothing."
Industry	"Lose no time; be always employed in something useful; cut off all unnecessary actions."
Sincerity	"Use no hurtful deceit; think innocently and justly, and, if you speak, speak accordingly."
Justice	"Wrong none by doing injuries; or omitting the benefits that are your duty."
Moderation	"Avoid extremes; forbear resenting injuries so much as you think they deserve."
Cleanliness	"Tolerate no uncleanliness in body, clothes, or habitation."
Tranquility	"Be not disturbed at trifles, or at accidents common or unavoidable."
Chastity	"Rarely use venery but for health or offspring, never to dullness, weakness, or the injury of your own or another's peace or reputation."

Franklin took these twelve statements to a Quaker friend of his and asked his opinion of them. The Quaker friend looked at them and informed Franklin that he'd forgotten one: humility. He "kindly inform'd me," said Ben, "that I was generally thought proud; that my Pride show'd itself frequently in Conversation; that I was not content with being in the right when discussing any Point, but was overbearing & rather insolent; of which he convinced me by mentioning several Instances." So Franklin added a thirteenth virtue—*Humility*. He wrote a four-word statement describing what it meant to him: "Imitate Jesus and Socrates." He then organized his life into thirteen weekly cycles, and for one week out of thirteen he would mentally focus on one of those virtues in an effort to bring his performance in line with his values.

At age seventy-eight he wrote in his memoirs, "On the whole, tho' I never arrived at the Perfection I had been so ambitious of obtaining, but fell far short of it, yet I was by the Endeavor a better and a happier Man than I otherwise should have been, if I had not attempted it." The only qualifier he added to this assessment regarded humility (which, you remember, was not one of his original twelve virtues). Of humility he wrote with typical Franklin candor, "I cannot boast of much Success in acquiring the *Reality* of this virtue; but I had a good deal with regard to the *Appearance* of it."

Ben Franklin first identified his governing values, then he made a concerted effort to live his life, day in, day out, according to those values. That is the exact process we will be discussing for the next several chapters. The *first* step is, of course, to identify your governing values.

Each of us lives his or her life according to a unique set of *governing values*. Lying at the core of who you are as a person, these governing values are things that are most important to you—for whatever reason. Because they include those traits and beliefs—like honesty and love and belief in a higher power—that are the fundamental building blocks of your personality, you may not be able to explain their importance; they're just important to you. Other governing values, like the desire for financial security or the need to make a difference, represent mega-goals that we feel driven to accomplish in life. Whatever your particular governing values may be, they are represented by the clearest answers you can give to these questions: *What are the highest priorities in my life?* and *Of these priorities which do I value most?*

Even though our governing values are our highest priorities, there often exists a gap between these ideals and our present reality. Our performance relating to those values is never perfect, but as our performance improves, something wonderful happens. We experience the inner peace we've talked about. Abraham Maslow referred to this unity between our values and our everyday performance as "self-actualization." *It is a bringing together of what I do and what I really value.*

Crossing the I Beam

I'm not going to try to sell you on a set of values. That would be both inappropriate and unnecessary. You've already got your values. But having them and identifying them are two different matters. Examining your life and facing up to your actual values may be one of the most difficult (though rewarding) experiences of your life. In fact, this is such a critical activity that I usually suggest to people that they spend five to seven hours analyzing their values and goals.

To get you started on this demanding process, let me walk you through a scenario, originally developed by James W. Newman, author of *Release*

Your Brakes!, that will help you reach inside and discover what these values are.

Imagine that I've come to visit you at your home, and I've brought with me an I beam that's about 120 feet long. In case you don't know what an I beam is, it's a steel beam that's used in construction. A cross section of it looks like a capital "I." Turn it on its side and it becomes an H beam. Let's suppose I've got this I beam lying in the street in front of your home. All your neighbors have come outside to gawk at it and wonder what kind of strange people you've started making friends with. But you don't care, because this I beam means money for you. You can put up with a few stares. You don't care what people think, right?

Now, imagine that I'm standing at one end of the I beam, and I ask you to take your place at the other end, 120 feet away from me. You walk to the other end, and when you get there, I reach into my wallet and retrieve a hundred-dollar bill. I have to shout a little bit—120 feet's a long way—but I shout, "Hey, you down there at the end of the beam. If you'll walk across this I beam without stepping off either side and get here in two minutes, I'll give you one hundred dollars." Would you come? Well, that's up to you to answer, but I can tell you that in all the seminars I've done, I've only had one person turn me down. I'll tell you about him in a minute.

Now I'm going to change the scenario a little bit. I'm going to take this I beam and put it on the back of a long flatbed truck, and we're going to drive this truck to New York City. Down in lower Manhattan are two buildings called the World Trade Center—the highest twin towers in the world, 1,360 feet above the pavement. I have mounted on one of those buildings a crane that will let a cable down, pick the I beam up off the truck, lift it between the two buildings, and set it on the edge of each building. The beam is just long enough to allow about twelve inches extra on each side. Now, just to make sure it doesn't fall, I'm going to bolt the I beam to a little bracket on each building. Because of the expanse between these two buildings, the I beam is bowed just a little, almost imperceptibly. I beams aren't supposed to bow, but this one bows just a little, and it's raining. It's not raining very hard; it's kind of a thick mist.

Now, if you've been to the top of the World Trade Center, you know that there's always a wind up there. But there's also a wonderful view. Let's imagine that you're on one building, I'm on the other, the wind's blowing about forty miles per hour, and I shout through the mist and the wind and say, "Listen, if you'll walk—not crawl—across this I beam and get here in two minutes, I'll give you one hundred dollars." Would you come now? If you would, you'd be the first person I've ever met who would come across the I beam for one hundred dollars. In fact, I've yet to find someone who will come across for one thousand or ten thousand or one hundred thousand dollars. At $1 million (tax-free, of course) some hesitate before turning me down. Now, why won't people cross the I beam for all that money? For the simple reason that they value life more than they value the money.

Now, let's change the scenario again. I'm not a nice guy anymore. You have a two-year-old daughter, but I've kidnapped her and I'm holding her by the hair over the edge on my side, and I say, "Listen, if you don't get across that I beam right now, I'll drop your daughter." Would you come now?

As I use this imaginary scenario in my seminars, it's incredible to see people's faces when I hold the two-year-old over the edge. Suddenly they understand what I'm driving at. When the scenario becomes very personal, the concept of personal values becomes incredibly clear, and we realize that there are very few things for which we would cross the I beam. We understand, perhaps for the first time, just how much we value our own life. But we also realize that there are a few things that are more important to us than our own life. A two-year-old daughter or son is one of them. That is a governing value. "I love my child" is the most powerful value for many people. And when we understand that, the implications of that statement start to strike home. Money has value, safety has value, but love of a child has a far greater value. And love of a child goes far beyond walking across an I beam to save his or her life. It means more than risking your life for that child—it means living your life for that child.

Once at a seminar in San Diego, I made the mistake of choosing a woman who had a teenager to participate in this role play. I learned an interesting lesson that day. People will not necessarily come across for teenagers. I had the kid over the edge. I told her to come across. She said, "Drop him." It ruined my entire presentation.

The effects of this exercise are sometimes electrifying. Several years ago I was teaching this concept to a group of about sixty-five. When I got to the point of identifying our governing values, I asked someone to help, as I always do. And since that experience in San Diego, I always ask for someone who has a two-year-old. On this particular day a woman raised her hand. I took her through the whole I beam scenario, I had her on top of the World Trade Center, and I said, "Would you come across for one hundred dollars?"

"No," she answered.

"Would you come across for ten thousand dollars?"

"No."

"Would you come across for fifty thousand dollars?"

"No."

"One million?"

"No."

Then I said, as I always do, "I have your two-year-old child hanging over the edge on my side. If you don't get across that I beam right now, I'm going to drop your child."

Ninety-nine times out of a hundred, the response from the person I have selected is instantaneous—"Of course I'd come across." And the minute they say that, I have made my point. I have identified one of their governing values. On this occasion, however, when this woman was confronted with the death of her two-year-old, she didn't respond immediately. She sat there stunned, unable to speak. You can imagine what happened in the room. Everyone began to be very uncomfortable. They all wanted to respond for her, "Of course, go across the I beam. Save the child." But finally, after a long silence, this woman looked at me, very distraught, and said, "No, I don't think I would come across." The whole group was stunned.

She felt she should offer a reason for her unexpected response, so she said, "You need to understand, I have eleven other children. If I were to give my life for my two-year-old, who would take care of my eleven other children?" That took some of the tension out of the room. Many people— I could see it in their eyes—thought that was okay. Maybe.

I was able to salvage my point that day, and we proceeded with the seminar, but I could tell that this woman was devastated by what had just happened. She wept silently for most of the seminar, and didn't hear a thing I said for the rest of the day. It was a very uncomfortable experience for both of us. At the end of the seminar, she approached me with her husband, who was attending with her. She said, "I need to share something with you that I have had to face here for the first time. You need to understand, Hyrum, that the two-year-old child you were going to drop over the edge is a Down's syndrome baby. You made me face the fact that I don't love that child as much as I love my other children. That has devastated me." She continued, "I think I would have come across immediately for any of my other children. I have had a very difficult time loving this baby who has severe mental problems."

This woman had been driven to the very core of her life. Her values had been laid bare to her eyes, and she didn't like what she found. This is an important point, because having your values exposed like that causes you to evaluate them, reconsider them, perhaps change some of them. Up to this point she had without doubt treated the Down's child differently, even if she hadn't consciously realized it. She had a basic value that said, "I love my other eleven children more than the Down's child." That principle had been operating at the subconscious level until we unearthed it that day, but without doubt it had been affecting her behavior. Now that she had become aware of it, though, she was in a position to change it, and at the same time change her behavior.

Finding the Sense of Urgency

Not long after that experience, I found myself in Hong Kong, teaching about eighty-five people in a public seminar sponsored by Dow Chemical. Teaching this principle in foreign countries is interesting because of the different cultures and different perspectives on morality you sometimes find. When I reached the point in the seminar where I ask for a volunteer who has a child under the age of two, a man from New Delhi, India, raised his hand. I started with the beam on the ground, took a twenty-dollar bill from my wallet, and said to him, "Would you come across this I beam for twenty dollars?" He sat there, very reflective for a moment, then said, "No, I wouldn't." A bit stunned, I took him up to one hundred dollars. He still wouldn't come. I took him up to one thousand dollars, then ten thousand dollars. This man would not come across the I beam sitting on the ground for any amount of money. I said, "Well, I obviously picked the wrong guy. Tell me why you wouldn't come across for money." He said, "I don't display any kind of behavior for money."

I picked another gentleman, a Chinese fellow from the mainland, and took him through the process. I put him up on the World Trade Center, we reached the point where I had his two-year-old hanging over the edge, and I was watching the man from India out of the corner of my eye. The intensity with which he was watching me and listening to what I said was absolutely incredible. When I reached the point where I asked the Chinese fellow if he would come across for his two-year-old, he immediately said, "Of course, I would come across." I then turned back to the Indian gentleman and asked, "Would you come across now?" He responded with an immediate and unequivocal "Yes!"

I looked at him for a moment and said, "Isn't that interesting. You wouldn't come across for any amount of money when the beam was on the ground, but you would come across at 1,360 feet for your child. Do you understand the point I'm trying to make?" He began weeping uncontrollably in front of eighty-five people and said, "I understand what you are talking about." It was a powerful moment for everyone in the room.

When people have those kinds of emotions about identifying what really matters to them, something happens inside. They start looking at daily activities in an entirely different light. They start asking uncomfortable questions like, "Is what I'm doing today what really matters to me in my life?"

This is what prioritizing is all about. The I beam example helps people clear all the clutter from their minds and focus on what is truly most important to them. And when they realize how important certain values are to them, suddenly they experience a sense of urgency that wasn't there before. Activities that were always important now become both important and urgent, and when that happens, behavior changes.

Shortly after we started Franklin Quest in 1983, I was doing a pilot seminar in Atlanta, Georgia. We hoped it would open the door to six corporations for us; we had ten people from each corporation in attendance. This was a two-day seminar, and the first day we talked about governing values. Everybody was quite excited at the end of the day, except one man. After everyone else had left the room, this guy walked down the center aisle. He was so angry his face was ashen. He stopped about four feet from me, hands in his pockets, and said, "Hyrum, I did not spend two hundred and sixty-five dollars to come to a time management class and have religion thrown at me." I knew what was bugging him, but I was surprised at my reaction. In fact, I couldn't believe what I said to him. I looked him in the eye and said, "Hold it. Before you say something you'll regret, go home, ask yourself tonight if there's anything you'd cross that I beam for. If there's not, don't come back tomorrow, and I'll refund your money." He said, "Okay, Smith," and he stormed out.

It was an ugly experience; and I couldn't sleep that night. The next morning I was there at 7:30, one hour early. I was up front preparing my overhead slides, and this man came in forty-five minutes early. He didn't make a peep, but came down the center aisle and sat in the very first chair. The chair made a noise when he sat down, so I turned around, and there he sat, just scowling at me. My whole system stopped.

I said, "Good morning."

"Damn you!" he answered.

"What's your problem?" I said.

"There *are* some things I'd cross that crummy I beam for."

I said, "Yeah, I don't care what your background is, everybody has governing values."

Then he relaxed, and he said something I will never forget. "You know what, Hyrum?" he said, "I'm not doing a thing about any of them."

Here was a senior vice-president of the Coca Cola Company with its home office in Atlanta. He had found some things in his life that mattered a lot. And he was nowhere near giving them the attention they deserved. We sat down for thirty minutes before the seminar and for an hour after. In those two discussions I discovered that he was in the middle of a very ugly divorce. Attorneys were involved. I learned later that he left the seminar, wrote down his own governing values, made an appointment with his estranged wife, attorneys in the next room, showed her his values, and she was blown away. She left that meeting, made a list of her own values, they got back together a second time, compared them, and they were almost identical. Now, let me stress this—two individuals' governing values are *never* identical.

Not surprisingly, they put their marriage back together. For the first time in his whole career, his corporate life, he started controlling events around what really mattered to him. My point is this: *Everyone has governing values*. But those values are unique to the individual. They come from the way we were raised as children, from the experiences we've had, from our talents and interests and unique personalities. That's why I don't even try to suggest what values you should have. All I'm interested in is helping you discover what they are, and then using them to plan your daily activities. Why? So that you can experience inner peace.

Personal Constitutions

Exactly what *is* the Constitution of the United States of America? Have you ever wondered about that? The dictionary defines a constitution as a "system of fundamental laws and principles of a government, state, society, corporation, etc." It's the "etc." I'd like to talk about, but first let's explore the notion of fundamental principles.

In 1787, six years after the end of the American Revolution, representatives from the thirteen states sat down in a convention and decided that the Articles of Confederation weren't working. That convention was all about discovering the highest priorities and values of this new country. In essence, these men said, "We've just crossed a hellacious I beam, the Revolutionary War. What did we cross it for?" And in that convention, principles began to surface—ideas like justice, domestic tranquility, common defense, freedom of speech, freedom of religion, freedom of the press, due process, the right to a speedy trial, the right to vote, and the notion that a people can be united under a strong central government but still be protected from government abuses by certain checks and balances. And to make these principles and values clearer, they went through the painstaking process of writing them down in a form that representatives from all thirteen states could agree on. These written principles are our Constitution. And it *is* ours. The first seven words tell the whole world who claims authorship for this document: *We, the people of the United States*. No law is enacted in any state in this country until it is measured against this set of values for consistency.

Do you know which elderly gentleman had a great deal to do with the writing of the Constitution? Benjamin Franklin. He was eighty-one years old. And it was appropriate that he was chosen a delegate to the convention, because he had lived this principle for more than half a century. He had written his own personal constitution—his thirteen virtues—at a young age and had worked at living them his whole adult life.

I am now going to ask you to do the same thing Ben Franklin did, the same thing the representatives from the thirteen states did. You are the "etc." in the dictionary definition above. I want you to *write your own constitution*, a prioritized list of your governing values with a brief paragraph describing what each one means to you. Over time, as you grow and change, you will probably want to revise or amend your constitution, just as we have done in the United States in order to meet changing times and challenges. But the fundamentals of our constitution shouldn't change a great deal. That is why I want you to spend some time on this—it may take as much as five to seven hours—so that you're certain you've reached your core values and can then use them to guide your daily activities.

Quite frankly, the I beam scenario is a bit heavy. I've been to the top of the World Trade Center and looked over the edge, and I found myself saying, "Hyrum, there isn't anything you would cross the I beam for." But when I'm totally honest with myself, I believe that the first three of my sixteen governing values would move me onto that beam. So would the ones that deal with my family. The others are important to me, but not so important that I'd risk my life for them.

Now, to give you a concrete example of what I've been talking about, I'm going to share with you an abbreviated version of my sixteen governing values. Notice that I state these values and their explanations as affirmations. I am not perfect, but as I read my values, I find it helpful to imagine myself as I want to be. Just as an architect imagines the finished building as he is drawing and reviewing the plans, I imagine a "finished" Hyrum Smith as I review my governing values.

1. *I love God with all my heart, mind, and strength.*

   As the scriptures and the prophets have commanded since the beginning, I seek first the Kingdom of God. I exhibit my love for the Lord by living his laws. I pray often, expressing my appreciation and love for all I have. Most of all, I exhibit my love by the life I live and by my untiring effort to serve him in whatever capacity I am called.

2. *I love my neighbor as myself.*

   I recognize and accept the fact that all men and women are equal in the sight of God. I never do anything in any way to harm or destroy the self-worth of another human being. As far as I am able, I aid all people in their needs. Charity is my mortal quest, "the ability to separate behavior from the human being." I do not criticize anyone's beliefs. I honor the individual and his right to exist, think, feel, and believe the way he chooses.

3. *I obey all the commandments of God.*

The commandments of God are clear descriptions of natural laws of the universe. When I obey any natural law, I have a credible claim to the natural consequences of that law. I obey the commandments for two reasons: 1.) God asked me to, and 2.) they work.

4. *I am humble.*

The definition of humility that works for me is: The realization of our dependence on God. I recognize that everything I have, am, ever will have or be is a direct gift from God. Humility is not weakness, merely a recognition of my nothingness in the universe.

5. *I am an outstanding husband and father.*

I take sufficient, meaningful time with my wife and my children to help them in their spiritual, intellectual, social, professional, physical, and financial needs. I love my wife with care, respect, and kindness. I build strong family unity. I build self-esteem in my children and help them maximize their potential.

6. *I honor the memory of my father and mother.*

My parents gave me life, taught me the basic principles of Christian living, and set a marvelous example for me to follow. (My father passed away more than a quarter of a century ago. My mother died in 1992, and I made certain that she was cared for to the day she passed away.)

7. *I foster intellectual growth.*

A man can think no deeper than his vocabulary will allow him to. I read regularly each day. I select my reading from the best books and articles of the day. One cannot teach from an empty well.

8. *I am honest in all things.*

I am honest with myself first, recognizing that to be honest with my fellow men requires that I first be honest with myself. I listen to my conscience on all decisions. The Golden Rule is a natural law of the universe. It works.

9. *I use excellent speech.*

The ability to communicate orally is a gift. I never use profanity. I use the best English and grammar I know. When a concept is served well, people listen and learn.

10. *I maintain a strong and healthy body.*

My body is a temple of God that houses my spirit. Maintaining my governing values is not possible without being in excellent shape. I eat, sleep, and exercise in such a manner as to maintain a high level of energy. I take nothing into my body that will in any way detract from my ability to perform at my peak on a consistent basis. I eliminate negative energy.

11. *I value my time.*

A natural by-product of high self-esteem is an increase in the value of time. Managing time is nothing more than gaining control of the events in my life. In a period of solitude every day, I evaluate the events of my life for that day. In this period of introspection, I determine the sequence of events that will have the greatest value to me. Inner peace can come only when I manage what I do according to my governing values. I and my colleagues have developed the Franklin Day Planner to aid myself and others in this quest.

12. *I am financially independent.*

I have developed an income that will be present whether I am capable of working or not. My family's needs are taken care of in such a way that they will never be without food, shelter, transportation, or education.

13. *I have a period of solitude daily.*

The magic three hours, from 5:00 to 8:00 A.M., are practiced in my home six days a week (and two hours on Sunday). During this period, I teach my family, read, develop my plan for the day, spend time in prayer both personally and with my family. This experience is the beginning of inner peace for each day.

14. *I change people's lives.*

I teach correct principles and do so in such a way that people will be motivated to experiment with and utilize them. Once these principles are internalized, people will govern themselves in a manner that will bring greater control and inner peace.

15. *I listen well.*

I listen carefully to all input, both positive and negative, weigh it, and then respond with respect and love.

16. *I have order in my life at all times.*

I maintain a sense of order in all aspects of my life. My physical surroundings are always clean, organized, and structured so that they bring calm into my life. My personal hygiene is immaculate, as are my personal habits.

Now, as you can see, this is a tall order. I'm not perfect. I'm not even close. My wife once read these paragraphs and asked, "When, Hyrum, when?" But I've set my goals high. I can't help but set them high, because my goals are tied directly to my values, and the things I value are extremely important to me. If I can keep this vision of the "finished" Hyrum before my eyes on a daily basis, I will find it easier to *do* the things that will help me *be* the person I want to be.

Remember that these are the governing values I've identified in *my* life. To you and others, a different set of values will emerge as life's highest priorities. Here is a personal Constitution shared with me by a young working mother who attended one of our seminars and identified her list of governing values:

1. *I am a patient, understanding mother.*
   Long-range Goal: Happy, unstressed, loving children
   I make time for my children, taking comp time when necessary and reserving my weekends to spend quality time with them. I put myself in their shoes before I decide on discipline, and believe that I do not have to inflict physical pain on them when trying to teach them to do things that I don't think are acceptable. I love my children unconditionally, and I make sure they know I love them even though I may not approve of some of their actions. I don't sweat the small stuff and let it affect my basic relationship with my children.
2. *I grow intellectually.*
   Long-range Goal: Better education and larger fund of knowledge
   I listen with an open mind to what people have to say and take in what I think might enhance my world. I read things relating to all aspects of my life (job, kids, the world in general) and seek to internalize worthwhile things. I seek opportunities for formal education that will help me learn and grow. I learn everything I can about my department and company that will enhance my ability to do a better job.

3. *I am generous.*

Long-range Goal: For the memory of my parents' generosity to live in me forever

I remember the generosity of my parents and seek to ensure that their example will live in me always. I help people out whenever I see a need, and expect nothing in return. I give my kids time and love, along with little surprises.

4. *I love God.*

Long-range Goal: Religious harmony among my family

I appreciate all that God has given me and love him unconditionally. I talk to my children about God's love. I show in my own life that actions are more important than words when it comes to being a good Christian. I take my children to church when they are an appropriate age to appreciate what is being said.

5. *I am kind to myself.*

Long-range Goal: Less stress, more organization

I regularly exercise and keep myself physically fit. I make sure there is enough time when I get to work to relax and plan my day before work starts. I blow off things that are not critical to the happiness of myself, children, or husband. I love each day of my life and do not waste time on unproductive feelings. I concentrate on the positive in all situations. I have the strength of my convictions, no matter how unpopular they may be among others.

6. *I love and appreciate my husband.*

Long-range Goal: Harmony, happy home for us and children, "forever" love

I regularly arrange to have times of undivided attention for my husband (away from our kids). I listen to his frustrations without becoming impatient. I do things to promote long-term happiness between us. I am grateful to God for each day with this wonderful man, and I tell him daily how much I appreciate his love. I concentrate on the positive and minimize the little faults that can bug me.

7. *I am productive.*

Long-range Goal: More efficient, productive output at work and home

I realistically plan my day every morning. I concentrate on the things I need to do rather than just the things I want to do. I give my boss "his money's worth" every day that I work.

8. *I am financially secure.*

Long-range Goal: Ability to relax and enjoy life without financial strain

I make sure that I spend less than I earn and save something each month for a rainy day, no matter what. I contribute to my 401k plan and my IRA each year as part of my preparation for retirement and the future. I buy savings bonds for my children's college education whenever money is left over from the budget.

Here's another example shared by a seminar participant, written in a crisp, concise shorthand style:

A1. I am in good health.
　　1. I watch what I eat.
　　2. I take vitamins regularly.
　　3. I will stop smoking.
　　4. I will exercise more.
　　5. I will lose weight.
　　6. I am reducing stress.

A2. I have a happy marriage.
　　1. I communicate with my spouse.
　　2. I consider her thoughts, feelings, and needs.
　　3. I enjoy her company.

A3. I control my life (time).
　　1. I am spending time with my family.
　　2. I think positively.
　　3. I am planning future and everyday events.

A4. I am financially free.
　　1. We are planning our future together.
　　2. I watch what I spend.
　　3. I am developing opportunities for supplemental income.

A5. I am dependable.
   1. People can trust me.
   2. I am on time.
   3. I do my best in everything.
   4. I am honest.
   5. I am rock solid.

A6. I learn about new ideas.
   1. I look for new ways to do things.
   2. I listen to new ideas.
   3. I learn new ideas.

A7. I am secure in what I do.
   1. I think logically.
   2. I decide what to do.
   3. I act on my decisions.
   4. I am persistent to the end.

A8. I believe in God-given attributes.
   1. I believe in positive attitude.
   2. I believe in mental power.
   3. This makes me more confident.
   4. I can do anything I put my mind to.

A9. I am efficient and detailed.
   1. I look for ways to do things better.
   2. I keep track of events.
   3. I keep good records.
   4. I think about problems and/or situations.
   5. I do things right the first time.

As you can see, the exact words and the form in which they are written don't matter. Your personal constitution is meant only to be seen by you and those you choose to share it with. The important thing is to identify your personal governing values and to put into words that are meaningful to you some descriptive statements about what those values mean in your life.

*   *   *

Now it's your turn. Take the time necessary to identify *your* governing values. This will probably be one of the most difficult things you will ever do, but it will also be one of the most rewarding. As those things that really are of greatest importance in your life begin to emerge on paper, you will experience a sense of clarity and purpose unlike anything you have felt before. And you'll also find that the act of identifying and writing them down will suggest many things that will start you on the road to doing something about those values.

To help you, here's a list of governing values that resulted from a nationwide survey conducted in 1992 by Franklin Quest Co. We asked people to identify those things of highest priority in their lives. While everyone had his or her own way of describing these values, the answers taken together clearly grouped themselves into the categories listed below. The results represent a cross section of those things people across America feel are of greatest importance and value in their lives. They are ranked according to the number of responses received for a particular category.

1. Spouse
2. Financial security
3. Personal health and fitness
4. Children and family
5. Spirituality/Religion
6. A sense of accomplishment
7. Integrity and honesty
8. Occupational satisfaction
9. Love for others/Service
10. Education and learning
11. Self-respect
12. Taking responsibility
13. Exercising leadership
14. Inner harmony
15. Independence
16. Intelligence and wisdom
17. Understanding
18. Quality of life
19. Happiness/Positive attitude
20. Pleasure

21. Self-control
22. Ambition
23. Being capable
24. Imagination and creativity
25. Forgiveness
26. Generosity
27. Equality
28. Friendship
29. Beauty
30. Courage

The survey was done to assist us in the development of *ValuesQuest*™, a software package for personal computers that is designed to help people identify their governing values and define long-range goals to fully implement those governing values in their lives. The software will walk you through the process and help you organize your own personal constitution. (If you have a PC, this interactive software may be helpful. For more information about *ValuesQuest*, or about Franklin Quest's videocassette, *Finding Your Values, Reaching Your Goals*, call the toll-free number listed at the end of this book.)

Remember that your governing values are yours alone, so don't feel that you must be restricted to those values on the list. If something else is important to you, it's important. You don't have to defend it to me or anyone else. There are no "incorrect" answers.

Once you've identified your unique set of governing values, you've built the foundation of your personal productivity pyramid (or fulfillment pyramid, if you prefer), the larger framework in which your governing values, long-range and intermediate goals, and daily activities can all be focused to help you achieve the thing we all desire in life: inner peace. We'll talk about the pyramid and the importance of prioritizing your governing values in Law 3.

LAW 3

When your daily activities reflect your governing values, you experience inner peace

In the introductory chapter of this book I told you about the Merrill Lynch executive who wrote to me after the untimely death of his son. Because he had identified his governing values and had done something about them, he was able to experience a degree of inner peace despite this tragedy in his life. He had come face-to-face with what mattered in his life, and he had chosen to do something about it. In other words, he took control of his life. Then, when tragedy occurred, he didn't have to go through the guilt that so many experience.

I have received many letters of the other kind, letters from dads who have stood in the wedding reception line of a daughter or son and wept because they never took that child to the football game as they had promised, never played catch, never went fishing, never drove into town for banana splits, never did a hundred things they had always intended to do—because they were always out of town or were too busy. Now they realize that the window of opportunity has closed, so they weep at the wedding. It's not that they're particularly sad about the wedding; they're sad about all the things they could have done, should have done, and didn't.

The same could apply to either a father or mother with a child of either gender. Discovering what's most important to you, and doing something about it is what inner peace is all about. It's that simple, but in a way it's the hardest thing in the world, because insignificant things get in the way, lower priorities that seem urgent at the moment. And, as we've already seen, important things are seldom urgent, unless we make them so.

The Productivity Pyramid

In our time management seminars we use a model called the personal productivity pyramid. In the larger context of our lives it might well be called the personal fulfillment pyramid. It shows the four main steps that lead from identifying our highest values to accomplishing our daily activities.

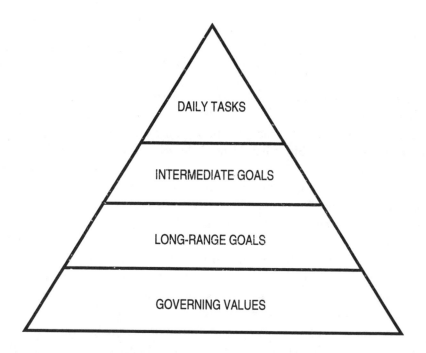

In Law 3 we'll talk about how to prioritize your governing values. In Law 4 we'll look at goals, the bridges between our values and our daily activities.

And in Law 5 we'll tackle the creation and management of your daily task list. What I want you to focus on right now, though, is the connection between these components as they are visualized by the pyramid. Everything starts with your governing values. If you set goals that aren't aligned with your values, you may accomplish a great deal, but you won't ever be satisfied, because you'll be neglecting the things that matter most to you. By the same token, if you create a daily task list that doesn't reflect your long-range and intermediate goals, you'll be *busy* but not *productive*.

There must be consistency throughout the pyramid. And it must be built from the bottom up. That's why most people are frustrated and stressed out a good deal of the time. They ignore the first three levels (and sometimes the fourth). They may make up a "to do" list. But they haven't based it on anything but urgency. The hinges that squeak the loudest get immediate attention. Consequently, at the end of the day, even if they've crossed everything off their list, they've largely ignored those silent, undemanding tasks that never make it onto the list because they are never urgent. They get the car repaired, make the mortgage payment, call the dentist, finish the report the boss needed at two o'clock, have a lunch meeting with a client, and put out a hundred brushfires at work, but they never get around to having a meaningful conversation with their spouse or taking the kids out for ice cream or reading a good book, because these things don't make it onto the list. Why don't they make it onto the list? Because, for most people, core values are not driving the planning process. This kind of day-to-day living is like a car without a driver. It goes wherever the slope and shape of the terrain encourage it to go.

We chose a pyramid to represent this process for a reason. The shape of the pyramid suggests a sharper focus as you move from the long term to the short term. It suggests an increasing degree of specificity. Governing values are, by definition, general statements of principle and belief. Long-term goals are created by translating those principles into what you want to achieve several years down the road. The long-term goals, in turn, are reached not in one magnificent leap, but through several intermediate steps. And the intermediate steps are achieved through a series of specific, goal-oriented daily efforts.

If your daily activities are guided in this manner by your fundamental values, you will feel the satisfaction that comes from succeeding at those things that mean the most to you. This satisfaction is a significant part of the inner peace we all desire.

The man who wrote me the letter about the death of his eight-year-old son took this natural law to heart and applied it in his life. He took the time to evaluate his real values. Then he planned his life around those values and, as a consequence, was at peace with himself in spite of the terrible grief he felt. He had earned the right to that inner peace.

The Importance of Establishing Our Priorities

One mistake we must avoid is assuming we're finished building the base of the pyramid once we've merely identified our governing values. Identifying them is not enough. We must also rank them in order of priority. Otherwise we won't know which of our goals and daily activities are most important. For example, I have a value that says, *I maintain a strong and healthy body*. I have another that says, *I am an outstanding husband and father*. Maybe I've set goals to play tennis once a week and to do something with each of my kids once a week. Usually this is no problem. I can do both. But what if I have an unusually busy week and I can't fit both my kids and tennis into my schedule? Which do I do? Well, if I haven't determined my priorities, I might just do the one that brings me the most immediate pleasure. That's what most of us usually do. But you may have noticed that I have already decided which is most important to me. Being a good father is value number 5 on my list. Being physically fit is number 10. I do something with the kids. I don't even have to think about it. I've already made that decision. When did I make that decision? Well, I made it when I sat down and created my list of governing values.

If we don't prioritize those values, we inevitably wind up with conflicting goals and daily activities and the constant need to make perplexing decisions. Let me illustrate with another example. Two other values on my list are: *I am financially independent*, and *I am honest in all things*. Now, let's assume I'm struggling financially. Let's also assume someone approaches me with an opportunity that's one hundred percent certain to guarantee my family the long-term financial security they lack. There's one little hitch, though. You guessed it—this opportunity isn't exactly legal, and even though I probably won't get caught, it's not at all ethical. What do I do? Well, it depends on which value is more important to me. If you look on my list, you'll notice that *I am financially independent* is my twelfth value. *I am honest in all things* is number 8. What this means is that I want to be financially independent—but only if I don't have to buy that financial independence with dishonesty. In other words, being honest is more important to me than being financially secure.

The point I'm trying to make here is that if you don't rank your values, if you are uncertain about what is really most important to you, you may find yourself having to decide on the spot between two courses of action that may or may not bring you inner peace. This is usually where rationalization and compromise enter the picture. When you are not certain what your priorities are, it's easy to rationalize. "Well, my family is important to me. With this money I could give them the security they deserve." Uncertain priorities lead to situations in which actions are not determined by values or principles, but by the desirable ends they may produce. We usually call this "the end justifying the means." It happens all the time. And the only cure for it is to clarify in your own mind the priority or ranking of your governing values.

Herman Krannert

In 1925 there was a man in Indianapolis, Indiana, by the name of Herman Krannert, an executive of the Sefton Container Company. On one occasion he was summoned to Chicago to have lunch with the president. He was very excited, because he had never been invited to do that before. He came to Chicago, went to the Athletic Club, and while they were having lunch the president said, "Herman, I'm going to make an announcement in the company this afternoon that greatly impacts your life. We're going to promote you to senior executive vice-president, and you're to be the newest member of the Board of Directors."

Krannert was blown away. He said, "Mr. President, I had no idea I was even being considered for this. I want you to know I'll be the most loyal employee this company has ever had. I'm going to dedicate my life to making this the finest corporation in America."

The president was gratified by this and said, "You know, Herman, I'm glad you mention that because there's one thing I'd like you to remember. As a member of the Board of Directors you will vote *exactly* the way I tell you to."

That took the wind out Krannert's sails, and he said he wasn't sure he could do that.

"Come on, Herman, that's the way it is in the business world. I'm putting you on the Board of Directors. You'll do what I tell you. Right?"

The more he thought about that, the angrier he became. At the end of lunch he stood up and said, "Mr. President, I need you to understand I cannot accept this promotion. I will not be a puppet for anybody on a Board of Directors." Then he added, "Not only that, but I won't work for a company where such demands are made. I quit."

He came back to Indianapolis that night, approached his wife, and said, "You'll be excited to know that today I was promoted to senior executive vice-president, made a member of the Board of Directors, and I quit."

She said, "You quit? Have you lost your mind?"

But when he told her what had happened, she was very supportive and said, "Well, I guess we'll have to find something else."

Four nights later a knock came at his door. Six senior executives from his company burst through the door, all excited. "Herman, we heard what happened the other day. We think that's the greatest thing we've ever heard. In fact, we quit too."

"What do you mean, you quit too?" he said.

"Yeah, we quit too, and here's the good news. We're going to go to work for you!"

"How are you going to work for me? I don't even have a job."

They said, "Oh, we figure you'll find something, and when you do we're going to work for you."

That night those seven people sat down at Herman Krannert's dining room table and created the Inland Container Corporation. That empire exists because a guy in 1925 not only knew what his governing values were—one of them was loyalty, another was integrity—but he had prioritized them. Suppose he had changed the order of those two values? Would it have affected his decision? Tremendously. That's why I emphasize that *this is the most important list you will ever prioritize.*

Choosing Between Two Positives

Sometimes not knowing the priority of our values leads to a different kind of situation—one in which both courses are favorable. Instead of having to choose between the lesser of two evils, we end up trying to choose between the greater of two goods. And only a clear definition of our values can help us determine which is better. Let's say, for instance, that your uncle dies and leaves you five thousand dollars. You'd really like to use the money to buy a new used car, because the one you drive to work now is falling apart and, besides, it's the ugliest car on the block. But for years now you've always promised yourself, if you ever got some extra cash, that you'd take your spouse on a second honeymoon to Europe. What do you do? You need a new car, but the trip to Europe would do wonders for your marriage and provide marvelous memories for a lifetime. Well, the only way to make this decision is to examine it in light of your values. If you have ranked your relationship with your spouse higher in priority than looking good with the neighbors, you'll probably be on your way to Europe, but if providing adequate income for your family is a top value priority and your undependable car is affecting your ability to do that, you may opt for a better car and find other ways to build the spousal relationship. The key is in making the decision based on which value is most important, not on the whim of the moment.

Choosing Careers

If you were to divide your life into categories according to where you spend your time, the largest category would likely be career. The average person spends more than eighty thousand hours at work. That's an immense investment of time. And, in the context of this natural law, work is also an area where many people experience a conflict between what they do eight hours a day, five days a week, and what they really value. This is one reason why so many people get stressed out at work. They're doing something they don't really want to be doing.

A member of the faculty at one business school discovered, after talking with his students, that many of them were majoring in business for some rather questionable reasons. These students were stepping onto a career path, he realized, that would not bring them the happiness they desired, because they were going to be spending the best days of their lives doing something they didn't really love. To learn more about their motives and values, he began giving his classes a simple anonymous survey that asked two questions: "Why have you chosen business as a major?" and "If money were no issue—if all jobs paid the same—what would you be doing then?" While there were always some students who were majoring in business because they really loved it, many students deeply and passionately would choose to do something else—being a schoolteacher, carpenter, social worker, artist, musician, farmer, dancer, writer, entertainer, coach, youth counselor, mechanic, policeman, pilot, landscape architect, tailor, you name it. But despite these deep feelings, they had instead chosen a lifetime of what may be very unfulfilling work in exchange for financial security.

If this last group of students were to go through the exercise of listing and ranking their governing values, few of them would probably place financial security higher than either happiness or doing something they loved—whether it was carpentry, coaching, or flying planes. But because they haven't identified and prioritized their values, their daily activities for maybe forty years will be determined, to a large extent, by false priorities. The conflict here between values and daily activities is clear, and the frustration that will occur in their lives is predictable.

Changing Careers

I've known many people who regret their career choice, and very often, by the time the frustration has simmered long enough to reach the boiling point, it's too late to go back to school and be retrained for another career. I have known a few people, however, who started over when they were already well down the path toward what they sensed would be a dissatisfying career. Clayne Robison is a good example. Today Clayne is a professor of music, but he got there the hard way. His story is so compelling that we used it in a video we produced a couple of years ago, *Finding Your Values, Reaching Your Goals*. In his own words, this is his story:

> My father was an insurance agent, so when I came to college I assumed that's what I should do. I immediately found some friends, and one of my best friends was determined that he was going to be a doctor. And he convinced me that the great contributions in the world would be made by doctors who

healed people. I decided, "Yeah, he's probably right, I'll do what he thinks is right." So I started to major in premed. I did well. I didn't have any trouble. In fact, that's the best year of college I ever had. But I was not happy.

I spent a couple of years in Germany, in the area included in East Germany. And while I was there during that period of time, I began to see that the real problems of the world are political conflicts, and if I was going to be idealistic and solve the problems of the world, like every young intelligent person ought to do, why, I should probably go into something a little bit more politically oriented. I could see the East-West conflict, and I decided I should help solve that problem. So I began majoring in English, and I enjoyed it a great deal. I then applied and was admitted to law school—and went to law school. But within five days, something inside of me said, "This doesn't really feel right. Something is wrong."

At the end of law school I took a battery of psychological exams that were given free to Harvard students, to determine why I disliked law school so much. A number of results came from that little session. One of them was that I see things very differently from the way lawyers see them. In fact, the counselor just shook his head and said, "How did you ever make it through law school? You don't answer these questions anything like lawyers tend to answer them." I said, "Well, I guess I was proud, and I didn't like what people would think if I quit, so I stayed." Finally he asked that critical question: "What do you really like to do?" I glanced over my shoulder to make sure no one was looking, and I said, "What I really love to do is sing." "Well, why don't you go sing?"

Clayne found himself at a major crossroads. In his heart, he did indeed want to "go sing." But that meant not only backing away from a financially lucrative career, but also providing for his wife and their two children while he went back to school to get a degree in music. From my own experience in walking away from financial security to follow my governing values, I know that Clayne's decision was not an easy one. Implementing it no doubt produced times when the family wasn't sure there would be food on the table. After long discussions about how to make it happen and with his wife solidly encouraging him, he made his decision and, at age thirty, Clayne Robison "stepped into music." And, despite the difficulties in making such a major career change, the contrast with his feelings about law school tell it all:

> . . . everything was fun, from that moment on. Theory classes were fun. Music history was fun. Writing my dissertation was fun. There wasn't a thing that didn't bring me joy in the process of pursuing that course.

When you hear Clayne sing or watch him teach, you can't help but see that he is deeply in love with his career. He also tries to help his students find their own values and avoid the mistakes he made. "It's fun to get kids to sing," he says, "it's fun to get them to make music, but ultimately, what I'm doing is creating an environment in which my students can develop confidence in their own emerging sense of what is valuable, recognizing that it's emerging, that it's going to change. It will be different in five years than it is now. But the important thing they're learning now is to trust their own sense of what is valuable, not what anybody else thinks, not what I think is valuable."

Tipping the Scales

The importance of tying values to goals and daily activities cannot be overstated. Whenever there is a breakdown in this process of planning daily activities according to core values, whenever the Productivity Pyramid gets shoved aside, you begin to lose balance in your life.

Before weighing scales were regulated and inspected, some butchers and bakers would dishonestly "tip the scales" in their favor to make a little extra profit. Their customers were cheated—because of the imbalance, they got less than they paid for. Similarly, people are misguided if they believe that "tipping the scales" in their favor by increasing the volume of tasks completed each day equals high productivity. While appearing to accomplish a lot, they usually end up burned out or unbalanced, cheating not only themselves but also those they want to please.

The key to maintaining balance is making sure our daily task list is built solidly on our governing values and goals. Some questions that can help us achieve consistency between values and activities are:

- What is the long-range priority of this project?
- For whom and by when must the task be completed?
- What can I delegate and to whom?
- Is this project more important than another?
- What will happen if I wait on this task?
- Have I included time for myself and my family?
- Are any of these tasks infringing on my values?

As we gain more control over our lives, we experience inner peace—which I defined earlier as *serenity, balance, and harmony in our lives through the appropriate control of events*. And that inner peace is only possible when the things I'm doing are in line with the things I believe. Value-based goal setting gets under the skin, makes people come to grips with what matters most to them, and guides them in planning their daily activities.

Many people leave training seminars with a warm feeling, but once back on the job, they don't change their behavior. Why? Because they are not empowered to change. Empowerment requires that people not only learn new principles and skills, but they receive a tool to help them implement those principles and skills. The Productivity Pyramid and the specific planning methods we'll talk about in Law 5 are just such tools.

In an unpredictable economy the personal productivity of individuals becomes paramount. I have a strong belief in the unlimited potential of people. That's why I talk about governing values, ask people to identify what matters most, and encourage them to allow these values to direct their daily activities.

What matters most in life should not be at the mercy of less important things. Unless we identify what we value most and put our everyday lives in line with those values, we will plan and live reactively.

Until you come to grips with your highest priorities—your governing values—you really won't have an overpowering need to set goals and achieve tasks—the upper two levels of the pyramid. But once you have identified those priorities, they won't just sit on a shelf and gather dust. They usually weigh heavily on your mind until you do something with them. That's the focus of Law 4, in which we'll learn how to set specific, measurable, and realistic goals—the essential bridge between your governing values and your daily activities.

LAW 4

To reach any significant goal, you must leave your comfort zone

In his book, *Release Your Brakes!*, James W. Newman explores the idea of comfort zones. Your comfort zone, of course, is a place where you feel comfortable, safe, secure. And comfort zones can be incredibly difficult to leave. In fact, it's a natural tendency for people to gravitate toward their comfort zones.

Have you ever been to a potluck dinner, where everybody brings food? Whose food do you eat at a potluck dinner? Very often, your own. Why? Because it's safe. You know how it's going to taste. No unpleasant surprises. You go to a cocktail party. Who do you find first at a cocktail party? Somebody you know, someone who's familiar, comfortable. There's another side to this idea. It says: If I can't get to my comfort zone, I will re-create it. That is why the recreational vehicle industry exists. I have a friend in California who had a motor home that cost him $130,000; it's the most incredible machine I've ever seen. That's Bob's idea of "roughing it." It is, quite literally, his home away from home.

Internal Comfort Zones

External or physical comfort zones are easy to understand. But they are by no means the only type of comfort zones we have. Sometimes we develop mental, emotional, social, or psychological comfort zones. These can be much more difficult to leave than our physical comfort zones.

A friend of mine (we'll call him Steve) has a young son (Todd) who is painfully shy. In fact, he is so shy that psychologists have a special name for his condition. He is an elective mute. What this means is that in certain settings, Todd will not speak. Todd is a bright boy, ahead of his age group in math and language skills. He is also quite uninhibited and talkative at home and at friends' houses. But in certain circumstances, he will not talk—not even to his parents. When he was in kindergarten, for instance, he didn't say one word to either his teacher or classmates the entire year. Not one word. And yet he loved kindergarten. The problem was that he felt overwhelmed by the teacher and the other students. He was thrown into a world beyond his comfort zone, and his response was, in effect, no response at all.

Steve and his wife, Sandy, were worried about Todd. They knew that the longer he went without talking, the harder it would be to change. They had heard about other children with this condition who were in third, fourth, and fifth grade and had never spoken at school. They wanted to break the pattern early, if possible. And the only way to break the pattern was to get Todd feeling comfortable enough at school that he would have the confidence to speak. You might say they wanted to help him feel at home. So before school started in the fall, they took Todd to meet his new first-grade teacher. They had requested Mrs. Stanley on the advice of Todd's kindergarten teacher, who said she was a very loving, supportive person, someone who praised her students and gave them a high degree of individual attention. They had primed Todd for this visit, told him he would have to answer Mrs. Stanley's questions, even if he only said one word, and expressed confidence in him that he could do it. They also warned Mrs. Stanley about the pattern Todd had perfected in kindergarten. In the end, it was enough. Todd didn't say a lot to Mrs. Stanley, but he did answer her questions. And that proved to be the turning point.

The first day of school Mrs. Stanley called on Todd, and before he could say anything several children who had been in his kindergarten class piped up. "Todd doesn't talk," they explained. But because Mrs. Stanley had already heard him talk, she was able to answer them, quite truthfully, "Why, of course he does. I've heard him talk." That simple statement changed the way the other students looked at Todd, and it also changed the way he felt in class. He talked that day. And he continued talking throughout the year. First grade became a very positive experience, and Steve and Sandy were ecstatic about the years of progress they saw in their son in just nine months.

Now, it's obvious that Todd needed to change if he was going to be successful and happy in life. He needed to leave his comfort zone. But it might be helpful if we asked ourselves what Todd's comfort zone was. Home? Yes. Home represented a physical comfort zone. School, at least during kindergarten, was outside that zone. But did he have another comfort zone? How about silence? Not talking represented another comfort zone, a mental or emotional comfort zone. When he felt overwhelmed by his physical surroundings, he retreated into the comfort of not speaking. And venturing out from his internal comfort zone was much more difficult, and more important, than leaving the physical comfort zone of his home.

Setting Goals

A goal is a planned conflict with the status quo. By definition, then, reaching a goal means doing something new, leaving familiar, comfortable terrain of our comfort zones and exploring new frontiers. Sometimes exploring new terrain can be adventurous, but quite often it scares us half to death. Sometimes we don't want to leave our comfort zones. Forsaking old, comfortable patterns can be one of the most difficult things in life. In fact, this is probably the main reason why so many people don't set goals. Goals usually push us toward new behaviors we'd rather not have to worry about.

Let me ask you two questions. What percentage of adult Americans do you think have written any specific long-range goals? Well, several years ago, an insurance company in Hartford, Connecticut, did a national survey. They wanted to know, among other things, what percentage of Americans had written specific long-range goals? The survey concluded that only 3 percent had. Now, from my experiences with tens of thousands of seminar participants, most of whom are successful professionals, I don't think it's that high. But what if it is that high? If so, then why is it so low? Well, I have a hunch. If I write down a goal and don't reach it, what have I done? I have failed. And in our society we have adopted a myth that says failure is bad. So isn't it smarter not to have any goals at all? We avoid failing by not placing ourselves in situations where we might fail. And if we remove the possibility of failing, what else have we eliminated? Right, the possibility of succeeding. Now, that may not be a conscious thought with most of us, but it's one of the subconscious ideas that keep us in our comfort zone.

Second question: What percentage of the American people at age sixty-five can put their hands on ten thousand dollars in cash? The number is 5 percent! Why do I ask these two questions? Because I believe they are related. Without setting specific goals, most people in this country will not achieve financial security.

In 1936, when Social Security was inaugurated, there were sixteen people in the work force for every one person on social security. The ratio today is less than three to one. Do you know what that ratio is expected to be in eight years? One to one, maybe. If I'm going to be financially secure when I retire, who's going to make it that way? I am. And I'd better have a plan for achieving that security, and my plan ought to start with a governing value that says it's important to be okay financially. If we don't set goals, we are just surviving, not really living, not to the degree we could if we took charge of our lives.

The diagram below depicts how we gravitate to our comfort zones. Unfortunately, it is a fairly accurate representation for too many of our lives.

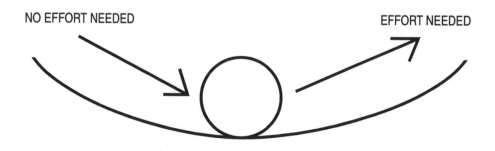

NO EFFORT NEEDED   EFFORT NEEDED

With no effort, we naturally settle into comfortable patterns and habits. It takes a great effort to escape the inertia of the comfort zone. Value-based goals are the force that focus our efforts and start us moving out of our respective ruts. And if we take our eye off the goal for any reason, we become unfocused and careless, easily diverted from our objective.

Time Lines

Have you ever said this: "Someday, when I have the time, I'm going to . . ." Maybe you've used that expression before, maybe not. But think about it for a minute. In fact, go ahead, finish that statement: "Someday, when I have the time, I'm going to . . ." Whatever you put at the end of that phrase represents a desire, a wish, a value in your life. Well, I've got news for you. You'll never achieve that desire and you'll always have regrets unless you do something about it. If we represented your life as a line, a time line, it would look something like this:

BIRTH   DEATH

There are two things I know about you. First, that you were born. I've represented your birth at the left-hand side of the time line. Your birth was an event over which you had no control. We usually just take birth for granted. But since birth you have traveled down your time line to the point where you are reading this paragraph. Find a pencil and draw a slash on your time line that represents today. Mark "today" on that time line. I once knew a seventy-four-year-old man who placed the "today" mark one eighth of an inch from his birth. He was wonderful.

As you look back from today toward birth, you can see thousands of events cemented into your time line—the day you learned to walk, talk, went to school, got your first job, got kissed, got married, had your first child, whatever. All of that is history. You can't change one of those events. If your time line were made of concrete, the concrete on the left side of your "today" mark would be rock solid. All the events of your life thus far are cemented into that time line, and there's nothing you can do about any of them.

Now, the second thing I know about you is that you're not dead yet. If you're reading this book, you're still alive. You don't really know how far away you are from the "death" mark at the right side of the diagram. But as you look out from where you stand today toward the end of your time line, you can't see any specific events. Nothing is set in concrete. And you need to understand this fact: The concrete on the right side of your "today" mark is wet, and it doesn't harden until you pass by that point.

Suppose that I sit down today and decide that one of my governing values is to be financially independent. I'm determining an event that I want to take place sometime in the future. But identifying that value is of little use if I don't get specific about it. So I look way down the time line and shoot an arrow at the date July 31, 2005. Attached to the arrow is a note on which I have written: "By July 31, 2005, I will be financially independent." I shoot the arrow and it sticks in the wet concrete. This is a long-range goal, the second level of the pyramid. Now, if I were to write a note that says, "By July 31, 1984, I will be financially independent," tie it onto an arrow, and shoot it toward that date, it would bounce right off the time line because the concrete is hard as a rock. My point: You can only make goals for the future. So don't waste time and energy on the past.

My goal for financial independence, you may have noticed, is very specific, but there's a lot of wet concrete between me and that arrow. If I'm going to reach the goal I've planted out there, I need to take quite a few intermediate steps. I need to ask, "What am I going to put in that wet cement between now and that arrow if I'm really going to be okay financially by July 31, 2005?" This is the third level of the pyramid, the intermediate goals. You know, I have people tell me all the time, "Hyrum, I've got long-range goals. Here I am. I'm getting closer all the time." But usually that's not true. They may have long-range goals swimming around in their heads, but nothing's going to happen until they jerk those nebulous goals out of the air, plant them in the wet cement out there, come back to today, do their homework, and start controlling the only increment of time over which they have any control: Right now.

One of the events over which you have no control is the fact that you're getting closer to that arrow every time you breathe. It's kind of exciting to realize you're aging as you sit here reading, isn't it? But if all you're doing is aging while July 31, 2005, draws closer and closer, you'll arrive at that date and you won't have reached your goal. Financial independence doesn't usually just happen on its own. Even people who win the lottery have to do *something*. For most of us, becoming financially secure is a process (like most things in life), and we have to determine intermediate steps if we're going be successful at that process.

What are some intermediate steps along the path to financial independence? Well, perhaps such things as getting some schooling and developing an investment portfolio; a job is always nice, maybe some life insurance or real estate. We've just identified five intermediate goals. Can we be more specific than that? Sure we can. Can we take the investment portfolio and identify thirty-five tasks that have to be done between now and that arrow? Yes. Where do those thirty-five tasks have to end up if I'm really going to be financially independent in 2005? On my daily task list—the fourth block of the pyramid. Now, as I sit down with my values and goals every single day to create my daily task list, in addition to everything else I've got to do anyway, what am I going to add to my list that really matters to me? One or more of those thirty-five tasks relating to my investment portfolio. Governing values get into daily task lists through the vehicle of intermediate goals.

SMART Goals

Values explain *why* you want to accomplish certain things in life. Long-range goals describe *what* you want to accomplish. Intermediate goals and daily tasks show *how* to do it. When you set goals, I suggest you make sure they are SMART goals. SMART goals are:

Specific
Measurable
Action-oriented
Realistic
Timely

Someone once said that an unwritten goal is merely a wish. Writing the goal forces you to be **specific**. If a goal is not specific, you will have a hard time knowing whether or not you've reached it.

You only improve what you **measure**. If you set a goal that can't be easily measured, such as "Be more honest," chances are you won't make much improvement.

Goals should always focus on **actions**, rather than personal qualities. Instead of having the goal "Be kinder to my children," write about specific actions. "I will not raise my voice with my children" or "I will spend a half hour playing catch with Tom twice a week" are examples of specific, action-oriented goals.

Goals must be **realistic**. It's good to aim high, but if we aim too high, we can get discouraged, and the goal-setting process can become just another fruitless activity. "I will make $1 million this year" is a nice goal, but it is not very realistic for most of us. But then, neither is "I will make five thousand dollars this year." Goals that are too easily reached are just as useless and unrealistic as goals that are too far beyond our reach.

Goals must also be **timely**. Don't set a goal for which you honestly don't have time right now. And don't give yourself so much time that the goal becomes meaningless. "I will obtain my law degree by December 31, 2040," is specific, measurable, action-oriented, and realistic, but it is not very timely if you are already forty-five years old.

Here is an example of a SMART goal:

MEASURABLE:
milestone event and date given

SPECIFIC:
states exactly what will be accomplished

ACTION-ORIENTED:
sets up things to be done

By one year from today, I will have completed a college-level course in beginning French at City University.

TIMELY:
time allowed is reasonable, but not too long

REALISTIC:
goal can be achieved within geographic and other constraints

Goal Categories

As my friend and partner Dick Winwood points out, getting started in goal setting is much like learning any other skill—sometimes it helps to have a place to start. The categories listed below are designed to get you thinking about setting goals across a broad spectrum of your life. Your major goals should, of course, build upon one or more of your governing values, and your own personal constitution may suggest categories other than these, but they may be a helpful start:

- Physical well-being
- Family/Spouse
- Spiritual/Humanitarian
- Financial
- Company/Career
- Company/Strategic
- Community/Political
- Educational/Personal Development

As you review the list are there categories that give your conscience a pang? Feeling a little guilt? It is not uncommon for each of us to recognize an area of our lives that has suffered neglect. If you felt any such feelings, perhaps that is an indication of where you should start your personal goal setting.

Below is a brief series of self-evaluating questions for each of these categories that you may want ask yourself as you prepare for some personal goal setting. These may serve as idea starters for your own goals.

PHYSICAL WELL-BEING

- Have I had a complete medical/dental examination in the last year?
- Am I involved in a systematic program of physical exercise?
- Am I at my optimum weight level for my height and build?
- Do I have any harmful habits that need control?

FAMILY/SPOUSE

- Am I spending enough time with my family?
- Do I spend one-on-one time with my spouse and each of my children?
- Do I help plan meaningful family activities?
- Have we had or are we planning a family vacation?
- Do I take business work home frequently?

SPIRITUAL/HUMANITARIAN

- Have I volunteered to help another in need lately?
- Am I living my moral and ethical principles?
- Should I attend church more often?
- Do I foster a teachable, humble attitude?

COMPANY/CAREER

- Do I have a plan for career advancement?
- Do I understand my next career step and how to get there?
- Have I communicated my expectations to my boss?
- Will my current career path get me where I want to go?

COMPANY/STRATEGIC

- Do I have specific production/sales goals?
- Do my projects get finished on time and within budget?
- How can I be more effective on the job?
- Am I building my subordinates?

FINANCIAL

- Am I living within my income?
- Do I have an ongoing savings or investment plan?

- Will I have the money I need to retire as I want to?
- Am I using credit wisely?

COMMUNITY/POLITICAL

- Am I aware of and helping to solve community problems?
- Do I actively support my political party?
- Am I engaged in good community causes?
- Are my neighbors known to me and I to them?

EDUCATIONAL/PERSONAL DEVELOPMENT

- Is my education and training well-rounded?
- Do I have a reading list of subjects to learn about?
- Have I been to the theater/art show/concert lately?
- Have I planned time for rest and recreation?

These questions are designed to get your thinking started and to test your emotional response to each category. Perhaps you felt at ease with certain ones and ill at ease with others. Because there may be a higher level of urgency to work on a category that makes you feel the least comfortable, start with the category that, according to your conscience, needs the most attention.

Suppose you feel the need to begin your goal setting in the educational/personal development category. You'll want to select a future condition that you would like to exist for yourself in this area—perhaps you already have a very specific idea. Whether you pick a goal idea that is two or three years away or one that is next month will have something to do with the amount of confidence you feel toward the task. Take time now to identify some long-range goals and intermediate goals that will move you toward one of your governing values.

Three Obstacles to Leaving Comfort Zones

The old adage says that "the best laid plans of mice and men oft go awry." We've all run into the difficulty of setting lofty goals as New Year's resolutions, only to see them founder within a few weeks. There are three obstacles we frequently encounter when we try to leave our comfort zones and reach our goals:

Obstacle 1: The invisible committee. Some of our values come from others—from friends, family, peers or superiors at work, people we look up to. We adopt their values and perspectives without even thinking. We may not even know the extent to which these values affect us. It's almost as if an invisible committee has come together to determine who we are. If your friends think that European cars are best and laughed at you when you bought an Oldsmobile, you might find yourself buying a BMW or a Saab next time you're in the market for a car, even though you'd prefer to buy American. If your father has always drilled into you that business and law are the best professions, but your talents lie in carpentry, you may find yourself an unhappy lawyer or businessman.

It takes great inner strength to stand up for your own values and live your life in harmony with them, rather than living according to the values of others. When my mother was sixty-two years old, she decided to get a second degree from the University of Hawaii. I was present when she was having a little argument with a woman her same age about that decision. The woman said, "Ruth, this is ludicrous. It's going to take you three years to get that degree. In three years you'll be sixty-five years old." My mother thought about that for a moment, and with the most wonderful look on her face she said, "Well, in three years I'll be sixty-five anyway." I came right out of my chair. What an insight that is! I thought. She didn't let this other woman's values determine her goals. To her, the next three years couldn't have been put to better use than getting another degree.

Obstacle 2: Walls. Sometimes we feel walled in by circumstance or by past mistakes, obligations, or perceived limitations. Changing course can be traumatic, because the longer we remain in a particular pattern, the higher the walls get. Sometimes it becomes easier to hide our true values and the goals they prescribe, pretending they don't really exist. This creates a great deal of stress and frustration, and it takes personal courage to break that wall down.

Clayne Robison, whose dramatic career change we talked about in the previous chapter, had pretty well walled himself into practicing law.

He had graduated from Harvard Law School, was thirty years old, married, and had two children. He could have easily convinced himself that his circumstances wouldn't permit him to follow his dream. Didn't he owe it to his family to start working full-time and support them? He had a Harvard law degree, for crying out loud. Going back to school would simply be too hard. I'm sure most people in his shoes would have tried to ignore the core value that kept nagging at him. But he knew deep inside that unless he listened to it and changed course, he would never be truly happy. So piece by piece he tore down the wall he had painstakingly built. He went back to school to study music. His spouse supported him in the decision and together they made the sacrifices necessary for Clayne to do this. And in the process he discovered what we all should learn: *It doesn't matter what other people think.* If you accept yourself and your values and live according to them, the world will accept you too. In fact, the people who seem to constantly struggle for acceptance are those who are counterfeit, who are not true to their values.

Obstacle 3: Fear of change. Sometimes we'd rather live with the problem than try to change. How many people know they should give up smoking, but are afraid to try? "I'll just take my chances with lung cancer. I'll beat the odds." What kind of reasoning is that?

As mentioned above, sometimes we fear change because we're afraid we'll fail. Fear of failure is a very intense motivation for avoiding goals. We'd rather not try at all than try and fail. What will people think of us if we fail?

The opinions of others often deter us from setting goals and trying to change. If we fail, people will think we're good for nothing. If we succeed, people may not like the way we've changed. Ben Franklin once said: "The eyes of other people are the eyes that ruin us. If all but myself were blind, I should want neither fine clothes, fine houses, nor fine furniture."

Don't Take Your Eye Off the Goal

In most situations failure is not the end of the world. We can pick ourselves up, learn from our mistakes, and try again and again until we succeed. In fact, if we are not willing to fail, we probably won't have the motivation to succeed. Failure, in this sense, can be a positive force in our lives, not something to be afraid of. There are some situations, however—and they are very rare—where we simply cannot afford to fail. Reaching the goal is imperative. In these cases, a healthy and understandable fear of failure can actually motivate us to perform flawlessly in achieving our goals. Let me illustrate.

In 1965 I was drafted into the army. I had a close friend who was drafted about the same time. He went into the infantry. I went into the artillery—for which I was grateful because the artillery rides and the infantry walks. The Vietnam War was getting hot and heavy about this time, so a great deal of our training was to teach us how to stay alive in combat. This was an important goal for the army—if too many lives were lost we would lose the war. But for me as an individual, survival was an absolutely essential goal. If I failed at this goal, nothing else would matter.

As I sat through the training, I began to discover some of the devices that the Viet Cong had developed to prevent me from reaching my ultimate goal of staying alive. One of the devices was called a punji stick, a young bamboo stem about as big around as your little finger. They would sharpen this stick until it was as sharp as a razor. Then they would soak it in human urine for three days. Because the bamboo was freshly cut, it would absorb all the poison.

The Vietnamese then located the trails where they knew American GIs would be walking. They dug pits just a little bigger than a man and about three or four feet deep and filled the bottom with punji sticks. These sticks were embedded in the mud with the points sticking straight up. The tops of the pits were covered meticulously so that American soldiers couldn't tell that the ground had been disturbed.

They did this because they discovered that the American GI, when he was walking along, would dive off the trail for cover as soon as he heard shooting. It was the GI's first instinct, a carryover from World War II training. When American troops first went to Vietnam, quite a number of our soldiers died in those pits. Sometimes the Viet Cong would just shoot in the air. Our men would get scared and dive for cover and impale themselves on these lethal little sticks. It was an ugly way to die.

The Viet Cong developed a number of other ingenious devices that were intended to maim or kill, and the army did its best not only to find better ways to identify these booby traps, but also to train the troops in how to spot them and avoid them.

The interesting thing to me, as I sat in the warmth of Fort Polk, Louisiana, soaking in this training and looking around the classroom, was the number of guys who were asleep. About half were sleeping. This was training that would be essential for them if they wanted to reach the most critical goal in their lives at that point, and they were sleeping through it.

One who did not sleep through his training was my good friend who went into the infantry. He became what the army calls a Green Beret. He was a career soldier. He went through jump school, became a para-trooper and ranger. He was an intelligent and talented young man, and he found himself going to Vietnam.

Because my friend had stayed awake in those training sessions, he developed an ability to recognize those punji stick pits and the other booby traps from twelve to fifteen feet away. He was very serious about achieving his primary goal, so serious that he devised his own methods for keeping himself and his men alive. He carried in his pocket popsicle sticks with a ribbon attached to each of them. He would go in front of the squad, and as he identified the trip wires and mines and pits, he would put popsicle sticks next to them. When the rest of the squad would come by, they would see his little warning signs. Because of this, he brought his men back for eleven months without a failure. His squad developed an intense love and respect for him because he helped save their lives.

In the eleventh month, however, he took his eye off the trail for just a second, and he missed seeing a three-wire mine. His foot brushed one of the wires and the mine exploded. That tiny margin of error cost my friend his life. There wasn't enough left of him to send home.

This is a sad ending to the story, but his death brought home to me powerfully the fact that some goals are far more important than others. This is because some values are more important than others. If you're walking along a booby-trapped trail in the jungle or across our imaginary I beam between the towers of the World Trade Center, there's no margin for error. *With some goals, you simply can't afford to take your eye off the mark for an instant*, and you most certainly can't afford to fall asleep. A goal set and then never looked at again will never be achieved.

Nothing Can Stop a Determined Soul

So, you've identified your governing values, you've set one or more goals that will help you do something about those values, and you are keeping your eyes on your goals. Is that enough? There's another needed ingredient: determination.

Are you determined to stick to your values no matter how uncomfortable you might feel? Are you determined to meet your goals, especially the ones that are tied to your highest values, no matter how difficult they seem? Are you determined to accomplish your goals, regardless of how much you'd like to slip back into old habits? If you can answer yes, then there's nothing that can prevent you from gaining control over the events in your life that can be controlled. Let me tell you a little story about determination.

When I came home from the military, my wife and I went to the university to finish our schooling. I also became involved in the community and was asked to be an advisor to an Explorer post in the Boy Scout organization. I was excited about this new opportunity and met with the boys one evening. I was thinking about all the great things we were going to do and the goals we were going to set. When I walked into the room, though, I found five of the "coolest" teenagers you can imagine. Their body language was speaking very loudly. It said: "I dare you to teach me something!"

I thought to myself as I walked through that door, "Boy, am I in for it." And I was right.

I said, "Hi, I'm your new Explorer advisor."

I thought they'd be excited about that. They were not. So I said, "Let me tell you a bit about myself. I'm Hyrum Smith. I was raised in Hawaii, and it's a great place." I told them a little bit about Hawaii, and then I asked, "How would you like to go to Hawaii next year? We'll earn the money together, and I'll show you what to do. We'll put a project together and we'll go and spend two weeks in Hawaii." Then I painted a picture for them. "We'll go swimming in the ocean, we'll go to the Polynesian Cultural Center, we'll go to Pearl Harbor." The whole nine yards. No reaction whatsoever. I finally had to ask, "Does this interest you at all? Would you like to go to Hawaii?"

Finally, one of them moved. He rocked forward on his chair and said,

"Yeah! And the year after that we'll go to the moon." And they all laughed. This was not a good experience.

I went to the man who had been their scoutmaster. I said, "I don't believe this. I offered these kids a trip to Hawaii. They laughed me out of the room." He doubled up on the floor with laughter. He thought that was the funniest thing he'd ever heard. He said, "Hyrum, there's something you need to understand. In the last six months those kids have had five different Explorer advisors. Every one of them came in and offered them some great trip. Nothing as ambitious as Hawaii, mind you, but none of those trips ever came off. When you walked in there and offered them Hawaii, it didn't register on their scope."

I thought about that for a week. When it was time for our next meeting, I walked through the door, and it didn't look like they'd moved from the week before. I stood in front of them and said, "Listen, guys, last week I offered you a trip to Hawaii. You didn't get very excited about that, but I'm going to tell you something. Next summer my wife and I are going to Hawaii. Whether you go with us or not, I couldn't care less. Have you got that? I don't care. If you want to come, that's entirely up to you." Well, they started to move. One kid said, "You're really serious." A second kid said, "What do we have to do? You have to tell us exactly what to do."

I said, "The first thing you're going to do is memorize a poem."

That excited them a lot.

"You're going to commit this to memory," I said. "Your ticket to get on the plane next summer is that you are going to quote this poem, word perfect, to the flight attendant." Then I made them memorize the following words from Ella Wheeler Wilcox's poem, "Will":

> There is no chance, no destiny, no fate,
> that can circumvent or hinder or control
> the firm resolve of a determined soul.

Well, they thought that was great. They couldn't understand half the words. "You want us to learn it? We'll learn it." For the next eleven months, every Wednesday evening, they had to stand up and repeat, "There is no chance, no destiny, no fate, that can circumvent or hinder or control the firm resolve of a determined soul." During that time we embarked on what turned out to be twenty-nine major fund-raising projects. We discovered in about sixty days that there weren't just five cool Explorers. There were seventeen cool Explorers. These other kids just came out of the woodwork. "I understand you guys are going to Hawaii. What do I have to do to go?" "You have to learn a poem." "A poem? You've got to be kidding." Seventeen cool Explorers. We turned those kids into the finest sales force that town's ever seen. We sold cufflinks, Christmas wreaths, fire extinguishers, cookies, a cow. We even sold a guy's boat—and told him about it the next day.

About halfway through we were a little behind our money projections. There was a rusty old D-9 Caterpillar bulldozer sitting out near the university. We approached the man who owned it. It had been sitting there for twelve years. "We'd like to have your bulldozer," we told him.

"What are you going to do with it?"

"We're going to sell it."

"Sure you are. I've tried selling that thing for twelve years. It doesn't run. You can't sell it."

"Give it to us. We'll sell it."

"I'm telling you, Hyrum, you can't sell it."

I taught him the poem. He gave us the bulldozer. We went to another man who was in the welding business. "We understand you can cut steel."

"Yeah. What have you got?"

"We've got this big thing. We've got to cut it down into little pieces."

"What is it?" he asked.

"It's a bulldozer."

"Nobody cuts up bulldozers."

We taught him the poem. He brought his cutting equipment. It took him four weeks, but he cut it into tiny pieces. Those kids loaded all the pieces in a borrowed septic tank truck. Nine loads. We took it down to a steel mill, sold it for scrap metal, and netted eight hundred dollars.

These kids started to believe the words of the poem. During that year, I thought it would be great if the boys could sponsor a really classy concert. So I went to Reid Nibley, one of the finest pianists in the country (who happened to live nearby). I knocked on his door and said, "Mr. Nibley, you don't know who I am, but I know who you are, and I have seventeen Explorer scouts who have never seen a first-class piano concert. We want to know if you would be willing to put on a benefit concert for us. We're going to Hawaii next summer."

He just laughed and said, "I don't put on benefit concerts for anybody. I'm under contract. I can't do it."

"You could do it if you wanted to," I said. We talked for a long time and he started to get intrigued about these seventeen boys going to Hawaii. I taught him the poem.

It must have had quite an impact on him, because he said, "I'll tell you what. If you won't tell anybody, I'll do a concert for you."

"I'll only tell the people we sell tickets to."

"You've got a deal."

He became so excited about it, he went to the first violinist in the Utah Symphony, Percy Kalt, and said, "Look, these kids are going to Hawaii. How about you coming with me and we'll do a first-class violin-piano concert for them?" Percy Kalt got excited, so he came too.

We went out and sold tickets and made $750 on that concert.

Two months before the trip I laid another heavy requirement on them: "To get on the plane you have to have a full uniform."

"It's not cool to wear a uniform, Hyrum."

"To get on the plane you have to have a full uniform."

Uniforms started to show up.

Finally, the day of the trip came. They had earned over eight thousand dollars. They didn't get one dime from their parents. Talk about leaving comfort zones. It put me a whole semester behind in school, but it was great. We got to the airport, and they looked terrific. Brand new uniforms, red Explorer jackets. One of their mothers had embroidered their names in gold. When the first boy walked onto that United Airlines plane, he handed the flight attendant his ticket and said, " 'There is no chance, no destiny, no fate, that can circumvent or hinder or control the firm resolve of a determined soul.' Isn't that a great poem?" "Yeah, that's great, kid." Seventeen times she listened to that poem. My wife and I were last in line. The attendant said, "Stop! Let me tell you a poem. There is no chance, no destiny—" She quoted it word perfect. I said, "Isn't that a great poem?" And she said, "Yeah, and we're thirty minutes late. Do you mind if we leave?"

We took off from San Francisco in a 747. Those boys had never been on an airplane before. We cleared the coast, and the captain came on the loud speaker and said, "Ladies and gentlemen, I have a kid in my cockpit. He refuses to leave until I tell you a poem."

We had two wonderful weeks in Hawaii. We went surfing, took them to Pearl Harbor. I almost drowned two of them, didn't try to save one, but he survived anyway.

The most exciting experience of the whole trip for me, though, was when our Explorers crossed paths with a group of eight Explorers from Nevada. They were the *cool* variety. They had no uniforms, wild shirts opened to the navel. They thought my group was a little weird. But finally, one of my boys asked *the* question. "How did you guys earn your trip?"

The answer: "What do you mean, *earn* our trip, man? Our fathers wanted to know if we wanted to go to Hawaii to get us out of their hair for a week, so we came. No big deal."

What happened next was priceless. These seventeen guys of mine gathered around those eight from Nevada and said, "What do you mean, you didn't *earn* your trip? Let me tell you how *we* got here." They laid it on thick and heavy.

That was in 1970, and we've kept track of those kids over the years. What they've done with their lives is electric. They learned something about character and about determination that year, and the lesson put down roots and has sprouted, matured, and borne fruit in their lives.

Twenty years later, we took those boys—now grown men—and their wives back to Hawaii for a reunion. Not all of them were able to go, but most of them made the trip. It was a moving experience when each of them stood up at the dinner we held in Honolulu and quoted the poem once more. We spent four or five hours together that evening, and each of them told us what they had done with their lives in the past twenty years. It was a very exciting time. They had learned a wonderful, simple, but powerful idea: Once you have done your homework, then nothing needs to get in the way of achieving your goals.

What this natural law boils down to, I suppose, is that I cannot give you the determination you'll need to leave your comfort zone and actually achieve your goals. I could not give it to my seventeen Explorers. The determination has to come from you. If you are not a person of determination, or do not become one, you will not gain control over your time and life, and you will not experience the inner peace we've talked about that is available to everyone who does apply these natural laws. If, however, you are determined to achieve excellence, to arrive at inner peace through identifying your values, setting goals and moving out of your comfort zones, and controlling the events that make up your daily life, nothing can stop you.

LAW 5

Daily planning leverages time through increased focus

I want you to do a quick mental exercise with me. Think about your last ten days, and ask yourself this question: "How many minutes a day did I spend formally planning any of those days?" Shower time doesn't count, neither does jogging or driving or canoe time, even though these might be wonderful thinking times. I'm talking about formal planning time where you sit down and consider not only the day's activities, but also your values and priorities.

If there is *anything* that I could get you to do as a result of reading this book, it would be to spend ten to fifteen minutes each morning planning your day. If I could get you to do that, you'd not only scare yourself, you'd intimidate everybody on your block.

Leveraging Your Time

Leveraging is a popular investment strategy. Simply put, it means borrowing money to increase the yield on your investment. Ideally, the amount due is paid back with interest, and you keep the profits. Costs are minimal, and the dividends can be tremendous.

Time can also be leveraged. Investing a little of your time in certain activities can actually free up time throughout the rest of the day. A daily planning session can act as a time lever. The cost is small—only ten to fifteen minutes a day—but you will enjoy many benefits all day long, such as clearly defined tasks with deadlines, increased focus on more important tasks, less time spent between projects, and a greater sense of accomplishment at the end of the day. Isn't that worth a few minutes of your time? Edwin Bliss, author of *Getting Things Done*, said: "The more time we spend on planning a project, the less total time is required for it. Don't let today's busywork crowd planning time out of your schedule."

Five Common Excuses

The reason I make such a big issue of this, is that most people in this country do not spend any time planning. They don't leverage their time. If planning is the key to control and if it's such a simple idea, why do so many people ignore it? There are five answers we frequently hear:

1. *I don't have time to plan.*

   Surprisingly, this is the most common reason why people don't plan. A national survey was conducted several years ago by a man named Daniel Howard. The study was written up in Alec Mackenzie's book, *The Time Trap*. It revealed that most people don't spend any time planning their days, and 72 percent of them gave this reason for not planning. They said, "I don't plan my day because I don't have time!" Do you buy that? Of course not. We've already ripped gaping holes in that excuse. What they're really saying is that planning is not as important to them as watching TV or reading the newspaper or sleeping an extra fifteen minutes. They haven't placed a high enough value on planning. Perhaps they simply don't understand the wonderful consequences that planning can have in their lives. They are content with the status quo, with letting life happen rather than shaping and directing the events that make up life. If you start your day with no plan, will you be reactive or proactive? By definition you'll be reactive. And you won't be in control of your life.

2. *I already know what I have to do. Why take time to plan?*
There are always routine tasks that need to be accomplished. Sometimes these tasks can eat up a significant portion of our day. But what about the things that are not so obvious? What about tasks that relate directly to my deepest values? If you truly ask yourself what you want out of life, what you want to accomplish with your family or career, many tasks will surface that are not a routine part of your day. For these types of future events, a daily plan is necessary—even vital.

3. *Planning doesn't work for me. I have too many interruptions.*
Most us have had the experience of walking into our offices in the morning and before we can even take off our coat, someone notices us and says, "There's Julie now. We need your help. It's urgent. Could you give us a hand?" Some days are like that. And some of us have more interruptions than others. Admittedly, interruptions are a problem, but, as we discussed in the first chapter, there are ways of dealing with interruptions, taking control of them so that they become opportunities rather than nuisances. In short, interruptions are a poor excuse for not planning.

In an environment where frequent interruptions are the rule rather than the exception, we need to plan carefully so that the number of tasks, or the time needed to accomplish them, is appropriate to the amount of time available. If your time is limited, break tasks down into smaller elements that can be squeezed between other activities.

4. *I feel "tied down" when I have a long list of things I have to do.*
No one likes the thought of facing an overwhelming list of tasks. The solution, however, is not to avoid planning, but to make your plans meaningful and effective, so that they give you more freedom. Remember, the list is not in control—you are. Be flexible with your plan. Occasionally we all need "downtime." It isn't absolutely necessary to have a plan *every* day. In an earlier chapter I suggested that if you want a feeling of power, let the phone ring without answering it. The telephone is a tool. Treat it as such. Use it well, but don't let it use you. The same principle applies to daily task lists. Your daily plan is a tool, and its purpose is to keep you

focused on your goals and priorities. But don't let the tool control you. View a daily plan as your ticket to success. It's a friend, not a foe. Remember, planning puts you in control, and a by-product of control is freedom—even freedom to occasionally take a break from planning. And you can take that break in good conscience because planning has given you the freedom and control to do it.

5. *I don't know how to plan properly.*

Welcome to the club. Most people don't know how to plan effectively. Many of us assume, because we make an occasional "to do" list, that we know how to plan. Nothing could be further from the truth. But that doesn't matter. Keep reading, and before you get to the end of this chapter, you may not be an expert, but you'll know enough to make you dangerous.

The Magic Three Hours

Now that we've discussed the reasons why you should have a daily planning session, I want you to stop reading for a minute, find a pen (not a pencil) and a piece of paper (the inside cover of this book would do), and write a personal commitment on it. Write it any way you wish, but the commitment is that you will spend ten to fifteen minutes every morning (with hardly any exceptions) planning your day.

Now that you've done that, let me ask you a question. What are you currently doing with the magic three hours? You're probably wondering what on earth the magic three hours are. Well, the magic three hours come every day between 5:00 A.M. and 8:00 A.M. Are you excited? Actually, I lied. *My* magic three hours come between 5:00 A.M. and 8:00 A.M. every morning. *Your* magic three hours might be 10:00 P.M. to 1:00 A.M. or *any* three hours of the day. Whatever you choose as your magic three hours, they make up that block of time that is generally uninterrupted, when you can focus on things beyond the normal urgencies and activities of the day.

The point I'm making is this: Somewhere in your day (preferably during the magic three hours), there is a fifteen-minute period of otherwise wasted time which you can use for planning. Planning time is one of those events that is bumping up against the right-hand side of the event-control model. We have absolute control over that event—if we value it highly enough. I'm trying to blow away this notion that "I don't have time to plan my day," because it's just not true. And the impact of seeing through this fallacy is electric.

Before we talk about the specific steps in effective planning, I'd like you to think about a few important considerations that should be part of the process of planning.

1. *Find a place that is relatively free of distractions.*
   Planning time is thinking time. Most of us think more clearly if we can have a period of near or total solitude. For most of us, that will be our office before the workday begins or perhaps late in the day just before leaving for home. If the office isn't a good spot, perhaps some quiet place in your home in the early morning or late evening.

2. *Review the long-range objectives.*
   It's easy to get caught up in trivial things and lose sight of our core values. Daily planning time is an opportunity for us to glance through our goals and ask ourselves, "What specific tasks can I complete, or at least begin, today that will bring me closer to my goal?" Make sure that every day your task list contains a step to help you accomplish your dreams.

3. *Make sure the number of tasks and the amount of time required by each is well within the time available in your day.*
   Many of us have a tendency to overplan our days. Consequently, we often feel defeated by our plan before we even begin, or we feel defeated at the end of the day because we haven't made a dent in our list. Let me suggest an easy rule of thumb. Do a quick review of the appointments on your calendar—see how much time you'll have left over for your other tasks. Then factor in another 50 percent to take care of the unexpected interruptions and urgencies that you can't plan for. Now plan for the amount of time you have left.

4. *Set specific daily goals for tasks.*
   Be very specific in describing your tasks, such as "twenty minutes on exercycle." Vague tasks foster vague responses. Listing vague tasks is like having a bow and arrow in the Sahara Desert. You have an arrow to shoot, but no target. Specific targets usually encourage shots that have a good chance of hitting something.

5. *Anticipate obstacles.*

This doesn't mean approaching the day with a negative attitude. It means quickly assessing the prospects for unscheduled happenings in your day. Try to foresee situations that could keep you from accomplishing your tasks. Then plan around them—or at least prepare an appropriate response to them. It's like doing a radar sweep of the horizon to see if there's anything out there that could destroy your day.

6. *Prioritize your tasks.*

This final key is vital. Even the best plans can run aground. Unforeseen events can leave us far from the end of our task list at the end of the day. But if we've started with those tasks that are most important, we can have the satisfaction of knowing that whatever we've left undone is less critical than what we've accomplished.

Laser Thinking

Prioritizing means determining the relative importance and precedence of events. And it is absolutely necessary for effective planning. Prioritizing keeps us from spending time on things we don't really value. It prevents the most important events in our lives from being victimized by less important activities.

I want you to think of prioritizing as *laser thinking. Laser thinking* should help you remember that during your ten to fifteen minutes of planning time, you are focusing *all* of your energy and power on the answers to these two questions: *What are the highest priorities in my life?* and *Of these priorities, which do I value most?*

Several years ago I tried to teach my children the concept of laser thinking. They really got into it. I was excited until I discovered that what they thought they saw coming out of the weapons in *Star Wars* were projectiles. I said "No, those aren't projectiles. Those are lasers, condensed light." My son said, "Come on, Dad, how does light cut through steel?" He couldn't have set himself up better. I took him and the other children to a big bay window in our home, got from my desk a big magnifying glass, and had my son put his hand into the light. Then I put the magnifying glass over his hand. It created a big pool of light on his palm.

I said, "I want you all to watch the pool of light." Then I started to move the magnifying glass ever so slowly. The pool of light on my son's hand got smaller and smaller, and all of a sudden he screamed out, "Man, that burns!" Then I repeated the procedure on all six kids' hands. We ever so slightly burned every hand, and then we set fires for two hours, and they were amazed at the power of condensed light.

Laser thinking is the process of focusing time and energy on your daily activities through the lens of your governing values and goals. If they are foremost in your mind, you will accomplish those things that are most important to you. My partner, Dick Winwood, illustrates just how powerful laser thinking can be by telling the story of a laborer who worked at a large company in Portland, Oregon, that dismantled ships for scrap metal. Dick says,

> One day I saw him at the store and he excitedly told me that he had decided to become a dentist. A dentist! How on earth was he going to become a dentist? That was my thought, but I nicely congratulated him and went about my business. A dentist, indeed. No way, I thought.
>
> Later I heard that he had applied to dental school but was turned down because what college credit he did have wasn't enough and his grade point average was too low. I figured that would be the end of it. Next, I learned that he had enrolled at the local college night school in order to bring his credits and GPA up to a necessary level. Would this guy never learn? Shortly thereafter I moved my family to Seattle for two years. Then we were off to Maryland for another two-year assignment. A year or so after that we were back in Portland again. From here you can probably forecast the rest of the story.
>
> Walking through a shopping mall one day I happened upon him. He looked good. Tall. Dressed nicely. I was reluctant to ask, but finally got up the nerve.
>
> "You were thinking about dental school when we saw you last. Did you ever do anything about that?" I asked.
>
> "Oh, yes," he replied. "I graduated last year from dental school. I now have a few months before I receive my specialty in orthodontics. It's been tough, but it was worth it."
>
> As I walked away from that meeting I mulled over the

wonderful effect that "laser thinking"—focusing energy on a future, planned-for event—can have. Once we can decide on what is *really* important and pay the price for it in time and effort, we can accomplish great things.

Prioritized Daily Task Lists

What laser thinking means in terms of planning is that when you emerge from your formal planning time each morning (or whenever you schedule it), you bring with you a list of marching orders for the day. Only we're not going to call this a "to do" list anymore. Have you ever used a "to do" list? "To do" lists are a lot of fun. You build one on Monday, and it's still good on Friday. When you're working through a "to do" list and you accomplish a task on that list, what do you do? You cross it off. It feels terrific, doesn't it? Suppose you accomplish a task today that was not on your "to do" list. What do you do? You add it on and cross it off! Why do you do that? It feels terrific, that's why. Do you know why it feels terrific? There's a biological reason. They've done some interesting studies on this—one day I'm going to find out who "they" are, because they do some great studies—and they've discovered that when you accomplish a task and cross it off, your brain produces a chemical called an endorphin that causes you to experience a euphoric high similar to the effect of taking morphine. That's why it feels terrific, and that's why we write tasks down and cross them off. We get addicted to the feeling. Anyway, you're going to create a list every day, but we're not going to call it a "to do" list. Let me tell you why. "To do" lists are maintenance lists. They're things I have to do just to keep my nose above the water. The highest priorities in your lives rarely, if ever, make it onto a "to do" list.

We're going to call your list a "Prioritized Daily Task List." If you'll start thinking about this list from now on in those terms, it will never be a "to do" list again. Yes, the maintenance list is going to be there, but other more important items are going to be there as well. Now, there are three steps in creating a meaningful prioritized daily task list.

Step 1: Make a list of everything you would like to accomplish today, including tasks that are not urgent. No value is given to any task at this point. You just let everything surface—professional and occupational tasks, family responsibilities, civic duties, church assignments, etc. Twenty-five tasks may surface in Step 1. When you're satisfied that these twenty-five tasks represent everything you'd like to accomplish today, you're now ready for Step 2.

Step 2: Give a value to each item on the list. This is called the ABC valuing system. This is not a new idea. In fact, this is a very old idea, but if we understand what each of the letters stand for, it takes on more power. As you go back over the list a second time, you put an "A" next to anything that is *vital*, that absolutely *must be done*. If nothing else happens today you're going to do the A's. You then put a "B" next to any task that's *important*, anything that *should be done*. At the end of the day, if your A's have been accomplished and you have some discretionary time, you'll do the B's. Finally, you write a "C" next to any task that is *relatively trivial*, anything that *could be done*. If you have discretionary time at the end of the day, after the A's and B's have been accomplished, you'll do the C's.

Step 3: Give a numerical value to each item on the list. You now go back over the list one final time and prioritize your A tasks, your B tasks, and your C tasks. Prioritizing, as we defined it, is the process of determining the relative importance and precedence of events. This means that you determine which A task is most important, and you label it A-1. The next most important A task you label A-2, and so on. Then you do the same thing with the B and C tasks.

So you come out of your daily planning time with a prioritized task list, a list that tells you which tasks you're going to finish first. Now, making a prioritized daily task list is a waste of time if you don't follow it. For instance, if you get to work and look at your list and see that A-1 says, "Talk to Jack about flaws in his marketing plan," you might be tempted to put it off. Jack is your boss, and he hates honest feedback. You know if you don't give it to him, it could cost the company lots of money, but you hate to confront Jack. So you look down the list and see A-2. It says: "Write proposal for PQ Company." That's a big task; it'll take at least two hours. So you peek at A-3, and it's a tough task too. Well, in about nine seconds you're at C-10, "Call Steve about tennis." You pick up the phone. "Steve, how about some tennis?" Good. Got my first check here. And the whole day goes like that. At the end of the day have you earned the right to serenity, inner peace, balance, harmony? No. Why? What's left on the list? A-1 and A-2, those tasks that you know have the greatest value. This is the secret to laser thinking. You focus all your energy on accomplishing that which is most important to you at any given moment. Everything else can be put out of your mind until you're finished with the most important item on your prioritized daily task list.

A prioritized daily task list is an extremely powerful tool, but it is an incredibly simple idea. One of the earliest and best known stories in business folklore deals with prioritized planning. It concerns Charles Schwab, then president of Bethlehem Steel. One day Schwab was talking with a management consultant, Ivy Lee, when he came up with this challenge: "Show me a way to get more things done with my time and I'll pay you any fee within reason."

Ivy Lee then handed Schwab a piece of blank paper. "Write down the most important tasks you have to do tomorrow and number them in order of importance," he said. "When you arrive in the morning, begin at once on number one and stay on it till it's completed. Once you've completed the first task, recheck your priorities and begin number two. Stick with your task all day if necessary—as long as it's the most important one. If you don't finish all your tasks, don't worry. You probably couldn't have done so with any other method, and without some system you'd probably not even decide which one was most important. Now, make this a habit every working day. When it works for you, give the idea to your management. Try it as long as you like. Then send me your check for what you think it's worth."

Some weeks later, after the idea had been tried and found worthy, Mr. Schwab sent Ivy Lee a check for twenty-five thousand dollars—an enormous sum in the 1930s—along with a note saying that the idea was the most profitable one he had ever learned. Schwab also formulated a plan for all Bethlehem Steel management, using Lee's idea, that was carried out under his direction. This planning idea was credited with turning Bethlehem Steel into the biggest independent steel producer in the world at the time. When asked by his friends how he could justify such a handsome sum for such a simple idea, Schwab asked, "Aren't all ideas basically simple?" Upon further reflection, Schwab stated that the twenty-five thousand dollars was probably the most valuable investment that Bethlehem Steel had made that year.

Tools for Daily Planning

Now, you can use a simple sheet of paper to write your prioritized daily task list on, if you want. But that usually doesn't work so well. You'll probably find yourself writing things that relate to your daily tasks on any slip of paper you can find—napkins, backs of envelopes, cash register receipts. These little pads of sticky notes are the worst. I know some people who have tiny slips of paper stuck all over their desk and walls at work, all over their refrigerator at home, on the dashboard in their car—everywhere. I call these pieces of paper "floaters." They just float around until you either follow through on them or lose them. It's a terribly disorganized method for someone who wants to gain greater control of his or her life.

You can get by with two blank pieces of paper and a monthly calendar, perhaps coupled with an address book, but I find it more reasonable (and easier) to have everything related to my daily tasks, goals, and values in one place. That's why we developed the Franklin Day Planner as a unified, integrated planning tool. It gets rid of the clutter, and it is designed with the Productivity Pyramid in mind. It is a custom tool, fashioned specifically to focus your attention and energies on activities that mean the most to you.

Some of the features we incorporated into the Day Planner design are listed below:

A. A place for a daily task list.
B. A place to keep track of daily and monthly appointments.
C. A place to keep track of daily expenses.
D. A place to record commitments made each day.
E. A place to write journal and diary entries.
F. A method of retrieving information that is recorded each day so that nothing slips through the cracks.
G. An address and telephone directory.
H. A place to keep values and goals close by so that they can be worked on daily.
I. A place to manage finances and control economic events.
J. A place for key information, so that it's always at your fingertips.
K. A planning calendar section that reaches six years into the future.
L. Six tabbed sections in the back of the Planner that can be tailored

for individual needs, such as: work, home, church, civic activities, direct reports, immediate supervisor, etc.

This system is now being used by more than two million people. Twenty-eight hundred corporations in America are using the Franklin Time Management System and the Franklin Day Planner. Significant cultural changes have taken place within these organizations as a result.

At the heart of the Franklin Day Planner are the daily planning pages, two for each day (turn the page to see sample Day Planner pages). On the left-hand daily page you can plan your prioritized daily task list, following the process outlined above. Also on the left-hand page is an appointment calendar for specific time-pegged events, and you'll find a place to record any expenses made for the day—a handy replacement for floating receipts that tend to get lost at tax preparation time. The right-hand daily page is made up of blank lines, but this page is the one that sets the Franklin Planner apart from other systems and gives it such marvelous power in helping us organize our lives. On this page you record notes from telephone conversations or meetings, commitments made, assignments received, addresses and phone numbers, even journal entries—in short, anything you want to remember from this particular day. In your next daily planning session you can transfer necessary information to future dates, or put it in other parts of the planner, such as the address-phone or key information sections or any of the red tab sections you have set up for special projects.

The Franklin System, when combined with an implementation tool like the Franklin Day Planner, can give you incredible control over the events of your life. Let me illustrate with a story just how effective that control can be.

On the morning of January 14, 1984, I was sitting in my office when the phone rang. It was the senior training executive from Price Waterhouse in New York. His name was Bill Keane. He said, "Hyrum, I've heard about your seminar through Merrill Lynch and Citibank here in New York. I'm really interested, but I want to see one before we get involved. Are you doing anything here in Manhattan that I could come and audit?" I looked at my monthly calendar, and sure enough, in late May I was doing a seminar in Manhattan for Citibank.

I said, "Bill, I think you can attend that seminar, but I have to clear that with Citibank first."

16

FRIDAY
APRIL 16

S	M	T	W	T	F	S
				1	2	3
4	5	6	7	8	9	10
11	12	13	14	15	16	17
18	19	20	21	22	23	24
25	26	27	28	29	30	

March

S	M	T	W	T	F	S
		1	2	3	4	5
6	7	8	9	10	11	12
13	14	15	16	17	18	19
20	21	22	23	24	25	26
27	28	29	30	31		

May

S	M	T	W	T	F	S
1	2	3	4	5	6	7
8	9	10	11	12	13	14
15	16	17	18	19	20	21
22	23	24	25	26	27	28
29	30	31				

✓ = Task Completed
→ = Planned Forward
x = Task Deleted
G⊙ = Delegated Task
• = In Process

PRIORITIZED DAILY TASK LIST

↓	ABC Priority	
✓	A1	Planning & Solitude
✓	B1	exercise
✓	A3	contract due EPS
✓	A2	go over contract
✓	A4	meet w / Cindy
→	B3	deposit checks
•	B2	call Ed
✓	B4	call Ellsworth Assoc.

DAILY EXPENSES

lunch B. Ellsworth	$13.53

APPOINTMENT SCHEDULE

Early Morning run

review contract
↓

8

9 :00 staff mtg.

10

11

12 lunch w / Becky

1

2

3 :00 Marketing Meeting
↓

4
↓

5

6

7

8 call Ed at home

Late Evening

• Commitments Exchanged
• Journal Entry
• Thoughts & Ideas
• Agendas (telephone, meetings)
• Conversations

APRIL

DAILY RECORD OF EVENTS

16
FRIDAY
102nd Day 283 Left
Week 16

1	Dr. Robert Banks called. Appt. 2:00 March 21st
	3rd and Spring – Suite 214
	bring insurance card & form
2	Talked to Ellsworth & Assoc. about
	request for quotation call mid next week
3	Allied Travel – Nancy
	Houston trip – United flight 269
	9:29 a.m.
	She'll mail tickets
4	met w / Cindy. Draft of report due next Wed.

Monthly Calendar

SUN.	MON.	TUES.	WED.	THURS.	FRI.	SAT.
1	2	3	4	5	6	7
8	9	10	11	12	13	14
15	16	17	18	19	20	21
22	23	24	25	26	27	28
29	30	31				

He said, "Hyrum, I'll tell you what. That's a good day for me. Why don't you just call me in early May and let me know if I can come."

"Bill, I'd be happy to do that. What day in May would you like me to call?"

There was a little pause on the phone. He said, "Hyrum, I really don't care what day you call me in May. That's four months from now. Why don't you call me any day you'd like?"

"Bill," I said, "I've gotta have a day."

"Well, okay, why don't you call me on the tenth?"

Now, each day in the Franklin Day Planner has a full page of note-paper reserved for it, so on the note page for January 14 I wrote, "Call Bill Keane on May 10." Then I said, "What time would you like me to call you on the tenth?"

There was a longer pause now. He said, "Hyrum, I don't care what time you call me on the tenth. That's four months from now. Why don't you call anytime you'd like?"

I said, "Bill, I've gotta have a time."

Then, with a little edge in his voice, he said, "Okay, Hyrum, call me at seven-thirty. No secretaries are here at that time. I'll pick up my own phone."

So I wrote it down. Then I did one other thing. You don't have to do this unless you want the detail, and this is where you start offending people, but I wrote down the time of day when we had that conversation—it was 4:30 in the afternoon, and I also wrote down how long we had talked—twelve minutes. It was just something to do while we talked, didn't take any extra time or effort.

Now, there I was on January 14. My Day Planner only holds three months of pages. Where were the rest? They were home in a storage binder on a shelf. But that's no problem. I'm never more than twenty-four hours away from my next planning session, and I always do my planning where I can have access to the binders where I keep future and past pages from the Day Planner. So, the next morning in my planning session, I not only planned for January 15, I also reviewed the notes I had written on the 14th. I always do this. And guess what I found? My notes from a telephone conversation with Bill Keane. I grabbed my storage binder, went clear out to May 10, wrote his name, Bill Keane, and what did I write next to it? I wrote "January 14." Then I forgot about him for four months.

Isn't that wonderful? I totally forgot about him. I had earned that right. I didn't have to worry or try to remember his name or anything about him. That information would be available and easily retrievable when I needed it. There's a feeling of peace you get when you know you can forget something.

Let's jump ahead now to May 10. At my house we all practice the magic three hours, and those hours happen to be between 5:00 and 8:00 in the morning. Five o'clock's a great time to get your kids up— nobody else wants them at five. Well, guess what I was doing at 5:15? I was planning my day. I opened my Day Planner, and I had about twenty items on my daily task list. Bill Keane's name was at the top of the list. I could not remember who he was. The name meant nothing to me. Do you think you could forget a name in four months? How about five days? But next to his name I had written "January 14." That was the key to finding out who he was.

I reached for my storage binder, looked back four months, and found January 14. And there it was. It took seconds. My notes told me I had to call him at 7:30 A.M. Eastern Time. There's a two-hour time differ- ence between New York and my house, and by the time I had looked this up it was 5:23. I picked up the phone and dialed his number. He was right. There were no secretaries there. He picked up his own phone. I said, "Good morning, Bill, this is Hyrum Smith. What time is it now in New York?"

He said, "Damn."

I then said, "You may recall we had a conversation on January 14 at 4:30 in the afternoon. We spent twelve minutes on the phone. Do you remember that conversation?"

He said, "Damn."

Now, this is a wonderful guy. He's a six-figure executive, responsible for training twenty-nine thousand accountants at Price Waterhouse. Do you know what his time control device up to that time had been? A yellow pad. He came to the seminar at Citibank, sat in the back of the room, and at the end of the day he came up to me, his new Day Planner handy, and said, "Hyrum, I've got to have two pilot seminars for senior partners this fall. I can't give you the dates until August. Will you call me in August?" He was writing like crazy in his new Day Planner.

"I guess I'd better write this down," I said.

"You'd sure better."

So I wrote it down. When it came time to call in August, I didn't get him on the phone until late in the day, just before 5:00. "Is this Hyrum Smith?" he said.

"Yeah, this is Hyrum."

"Hyrum, you had two minutes and I was going to cut you out of my will."

He had written me down in his planning tool, put me on his prioritized daily task list for a certain day in August, and gave me a priority. If I hadn't called, I'm sure there would have been no seminars. But I did call, and we've now trained over six thousand people for Price Waterhouse. Bill Keane has become one of my dearest and closest friends.

Now, try to translate this experience into your own line of work. If you're a salesperson, for instance, wouldn't this kind of control increase your sales? Wouldn't your clients have a more favorable impression of you? The planning techniques themselves are important, but I can't overemphasize the impact a well-designed tool can have on your effectiveness. Can you imagine having an experience similar to my encounter with Bill Keane if you're keeping track of your prioritized daily task list on a sheet of paper or a yellow legal pad or on little sticky notes?

Using a Planning Tool Effectively

There are six simple rules for using a planning tool if you want to gain control of your life.

1. *Take your Day Planner with you always.*
   If you don't have it with you, you'll end up writing things on scraps of paper and become disorganized. And since you will put everything that relates to your values, goals, and daily task list in this tool, you need it with you almost always. I have people ask me all the time, "Hyrum, if this thing's so important, what happens if I lose it?" I just tell them, "Listen, if you lose this thing, you may as well jump from a tall building, because it's all over." Of course I'm just kidding, but your planner should become almost indispensable to you if you use it right.

   Would you take your planner on vacation with you? Yes. Will you do a daily task list? Maybe not. I often spend the month of

July vacationing in Honolulu. I have to do two seminars. But I still have twenty-nine days left over. It's fun to go back and review some of my daily task lists for July. A-1—Planning and solitude. A-2—Blow the rest of the day. Those are fun checks to earn. The endorphins just run wild. But what will destroy a vacation faster than running out of money? Worrying about what you've got to do when you get back.

You're lying on the beach and that big project screams into your mind. You cannot stop that stuff from screaming at you. Or, maybe you have a brilliant idea for a new product and you don't want to lose that idea before you get back to the office. What do you do? You go back to your hotel room, find your planner, dump your mind into it, then go back to the beach. Kick back, forget it, vegetate the rest of the day. You can do it, because whatever it was that was screaming in your mind has now been transferred to your planner.

2. *Use only one calendar.*

If you've got things written all over the place—on a wall calendar at home, on a desk calendar at work, and in either a pocket planner or a more elaborate planner—what happens? First, you waste time, because you've got to keep them all current, all coordinated with each other. Second, you let some things slip because it's too hard to keep more than one planning tool current.

Sometimes executives ask me what to do because their secretaries are planning their appointments all day. I tell them it's a monumental mistake to let someone else have that kind of control over their entire day. *Never* give anybody else a full day of your time to schedule. Instead, sit down with your secretary at the beginning of the month. This takes all of five minutes. You open your Day Planner and say, "You can schedule me on this morning, that afternoon, that morning," and so on. Then you go to the daily pages and draw a line through those mornings and afternoons so that you won't schedule anything there before you check with your secretary.

3. *Commit to planning every day.*

There can be rare exceptions to this, but if you want to control the events in your life, you must use the control tool. A carpenter doesn't put down his hammer and start pounding nails with his hand just because he got tired of holding the weight of the hammer. Every now and then he will take a break from hammering, but he uses the right tool for the right job.

4. *Use a good reference system.*

Let's use a hypothetical example to illustrate. I'm looking to buy a jet-black Oldsmobile, and on December 5, a dealer friend named Bob calls me and says, "Hyrum, have I got a deal for you. I've got that Oldsmobile you wanted coming in next week. It's a beauty and I got a special deal on it. I'll give it to you for fifteen and a half thousand with an interest rate of nine percent. You can see it on January sixth at eight in the morning." "Great!" I say. But with the holiday season in full swing, I soon forget about our conversation.

Finally, January 6 rolls around, I look in my Day Planner first thing that morning and notice my appointment with Bob. I go to the dealership at eight o'clock, but my friend is out of town. One of his salesmen takes me to see the car, and Bob was right—I instantly fall in love with it. I decide to buy the car, and the salesman says he can give me a great deal on it: only $17,000, and the interest is only 10.5 percent. Those numbers don't sound at all familiar to me, but I can't remember exactly what Bob told me. Well, I'd be at the mercy of this salesman, except that I've got my Day Planner with me. I open it up, and on my January 6 page, next to my appointment with Bob Garff, is a little note, in parentheses, and that note says, "12/5." That's it, just "12/5." I flip back to December 5 in my Day Planner, and there on the right-hand page, under the name Bob Garff, are the following numbers: $15,500 and 9 percent.

"Guess what?" I say to the salesman. "Back on December 5, I had a conversation with your boss. We talked for ten minutes at 4:17 in the afternoon, and he said he'd give me this car for fifteen and a half thousand at nine percent." The salesman's jaw drops. How's he going to argue with someone who can tell him a month later the exact time and duration of a phone call with his boss?

You see, when I talk on the phone or meet with someone, I usually jot notes down in my Day Planner. Then, if I know I'm

APRIL
MASTER TASK LIST

PERSONAL	BUSINESS
clean out garage	attend computer training
holiday vacation plans	update database for mailing
rake leaves	Karen 5-year lunch
Danny's school play	
cabin for weekend	

MONTHLY GOALS	MONTHLY GOALS
appt. w/ Dr. Owen re: glasses	plans to attend mktg. conference
estimates on roof	order supplies
Marathon training	quote to Bob Evans
read to kids every night	

going to need that information at a later date—perhaps when I next meet with that person—I add a note, in parentheses, next to the appointment to refer me back to our last conversation.

Now, parentheses can be used for other purposes than to refer you to a date in your planner. They can take you any place in your office, house, car, or boat. Let's assume you have a project you're working on. This project is going to last six months, and you have a meeting to kick things off. Do you record notes from this meeting on the right-hand page of your daily planning sheets? No, because you don't want to have to go through your planner and search for all the notes about this project. You want to be able to find all the notes in one place—a project file. So, in this meeting, you do not write on the right-hand page, you write in a special section in the back that you've titled "project file." Then, if your boss asks you for a project summary first thing in the morning next Thursday, you turn ahead in your planner to next Thursday and write your boss's name at 8 A.M. And next to his name, in parentheses, you write "project file."

5. *Use a master task list.*

A master task list is a tool you use to remind you of things you'd like to do this month, tasks that are not high in value but ought to get done sometime. Let me give you an example. You're sitting in your office and all of a sudden a revelation comes to your mind about your garage. You can see it as clearly as if you were standing in it, and it's a mess. You know, you say, I really ought to clean out that garage. I don't want to do it this month or next month. I think I'll do it in June. So you turn to your June master task list and write, "Clean out garage." It feels terrific because it's on your list. Once or twice a week you scan your master task list and ask yourself, "Is there anything I can bring from my master task list onto my daily task list?" Toward the end of June your conscience tells you it's time to make that move. You schedule it the last Saturday in June, you do it, and you feel marvelous—after you finish.

6. *Use a monthly index.*

A monthly index is simply a page where you write things that may get lost in the shuffle. Let's say it's June 12, you're walking along the street, and you see a poster with a catchy little poem

APRIL INDEX

Date	Index to important ideas, events, thoughts, etc., that have been recorded
3.2	flooring estimates
3.4	vacation plans–Houston
11.3	Ross' work schedule
14.2	directions to Teresa's
16.3	vacation plans–Houston
20.5	Bob's itinerary
23.2	notes on Ellsworth mtg.

on it. You write the poem down in your planner (on the June 12 page, of course). What's not going to appear on any future daily task list that you'd like to be able to find when you want it? The poem. So you write on your monthly index a key phrase that will remind you of that poem when you see it, and next to the key phrase you write June 12. If you're preparing a presentation in September and you seem to remember a poem you once jotted down that you think might fill a gap in your presentation, what do you do? You search back through the past few monthly indexes—it only takes a few seconds—and there it is, on your June monthly index. You turn to June 12, and copy it down for your presentation.

You may have heard of Vic Braden. He's a wonderful man who has become a very close friend. Vic has a tennis college in Coto De Caza, California. A few years ago he called me on the phone and said, "Hyrum, this is Vic Braden. Do you know who I am?"

"Of course," I said, "you're in *Tennis Magazine.*"

"I'd like you to come and do a seminar for all my coaches here at my tennis college. Would you be willing to do that?"

I said, "Vic, I'd love to do that. What day would you like me to come?"

"Well, I don't really know," he said. "Can I call you back in a couple of weeks and give you some dates?"

"Call me anytime you'd like," I said.

I had no idea when he was going to call, so I couldn't go to a future daily task list. I couldn't even write it on a monthly calendar. So I wrote it in my monthly index. Six weeks later he called me back. "Hyrum, this is Vic Braden. Remember me?"

Oh man, I thought, when did I talk to him? I reached over to my index, scanned it, found his name, the page, turned to that page. This took just a few seconds. He had about eight words out of his mouth, and I said, "Hold it, Vic. I remember that conversation very well. It was six weeks ago at 4:30 in the afternoon, we spent three minutes on the phone."

"How did you know that?" he said.

"Because I know everything." Chuckles.

He was blown away.

You see, a Day Planner is not just a device to help you plan each day. It is a book. It has twelve chapters, and each chapter has an index so you can easily find anything you need to in it.

These simple rules can help you use your planner more productively. And you ought to consider these rules when you are selecting a planning tool. The Franklin Day Planner has been designed, of course, to make using these rules easy. Regardless what tool you use, though, it needs to be comprehensive enough to prevent the accumulation of clutter, and it needs to contain all the information relating to your tasks and other events. We've designed the Day Planner to contain all the information you could possibly need to manage the controllable events in your life.

The principles and suggestions offered in this chapter are quite specific, but they can be adapted to individual circumstances and personalities. The important thing is that you plan, that you prioritize your plan, and that you have a tool that enables you to execute that plan efficiently. If you don't do this, your daily activities will be severed from their roots, from your goals and values, and you will be far less productive and far less satisfied with life than you should be.

Planning is a simple idea that you can use to leverage your time, and prioritized planning is a tool that focuses your energy and activities to ensure that you will receive the greatest possible return on your time investment. If you use these principles, you will be more productive and will have a credible claim to inner peace.

Once you commit to following this program of building your productivity pyramid—identifying your values, setting long-range and intermediate goals, and spending ten to fifteen minutes a day planning your daily activities—then comes the real test. Making a commitment is fine. But keeping the commitment is another matter altogether. The choice is yours. You can settle for a continuation of the status quo (with all its frustrations and lack of control), or you can achieve the things in life you really want to. It's up to you. The only real variable is something called character.

Character

Character, simply stated, is doing what you say you're going to do. A more formal definition is: *Character is the ability to carry out a worthy decision after the emotion of making that decision has passed.*

Before I got into the seminar business, I was running the marketing division for Automatic Data Processing. I unwittingly developed a little ceremony that I went through every morning at about 9:30. I walked down two corridors into a wonderful little cafeteria and paid homage to a shrine: a candy bar machine. I'd slip a few coins into the slot and retrieve a Heath candy bar. Have you ever had a Heath candy bar? They're as close to heaven as just about anything. Well, on one occasion I was standing in front of my shrine, about to get my daily fix of chocolate, when I overheard a conversation. Two fellows across the room, obviously thinking I couldn't hear, were talking about me. "Hyrum's getting porky, isn't he?" said one to the other. I froze in midair with my quarter, put it back in my pocket, looked over to see who it was (almost fired them both), but instead stormed out of the lunchroom. You need to understand that at that point I weighed 230 pounds. That's thirty pounds too many for me (either that or I need to grow another six inches).

My wife had been on me for two years to lose that weight. You also need to understand that my wife is a wonderful athlete. She held the long jump record at her university for nine years, played on the basketball and volleyball teams. She's in great shape all the time. It drives me crazy. In fact, you remember the magic three hours I told you about? Between 6:00 and 7:00 in the morning my wife and I go play basketball with eight guys. They choose her first.

Well, I picked up the phone that day and called my wife. "You'll be excited to know," I told her, "that I'm going to lose thirty pounds." Guess what her reaction was? Regardless, I was emotionally involved. I was committed to that goal. But do you know how long that commitment lasted? Eight hours. What happens about eight hours after you make a commitment like that? You get hungry. You walk by the refrigerator, it grabs you, and you suddenly find yourself sitting on the second shelf, eating everything you can get your hands on. I learned something about discipline that day. Stephen R. Covey, author of *The Seven Habits of Highly Effective People*, has defined discipline as "the ability to make and keep promises," including promises to ourselves, and I soon discovered that keeping promises requires a substantial, sustained effort. Discipline is not something you can acquire in a moment, then forget about. You must develop the personal resolve to carry through, even when the going gets tough. That's when the power of habit can help.

The Power of Habit

We are all creatures of habit, whether we like it or not. Even though the inertia of habits often keeps us in our comfort zone instead of reaching our goals, habits per se are not necessarily bad. In fact, life would be a nightmare without habits. We would have to make conscious decisions at every turn. Nothing would be automatic. We would have to think about everything from brushing our teeth and combing our hair to driving the car. If all our actions were at the conscious level, we would be effectively paralyzed by the sheer mass of information we would have to process. We would accomplish very little. Habit allows us to perform thousands of tasks and routines without causing a mental overload. The only pertinent question regarding habit is this: Am I willing to develop good habits or am I content to develop bad ones? This is another choice. As the following poem suggests, we can make habit our servant, or we can allow it to become our master.

HABIT

I am your constant companion.
I am your greatest helper or your heaviest burden.
I will push you onward or drag you down to failure.
I am completely at your command.
Half the things you do, you might just as well turn over to me,
And I will be able to do them quickly and correctly.
I am easily managed; you must merely be firm with me.
Show me exactly how you want something done,
And after a few lessons I will do it automatically.
I am the servant of all great men
And, alas, of all failures as well.

Those who are great, I have made great.
Those who are failures, I have made failures.
I am not a machine, though I work with all the precision of a machine
Plus the intelligence of a man.
You may run me for profit, or run me for ruin;
It makes no difference to me.
Take me, train me, be firm with me
And I will put the world at your feet.
Be easy with me, and I will destroy you.
Who am I?
I am HABIT!

—AUTHOR UNKNOWN

Developing good habits, in every area from diet to communication skills, can be viewed as a conscious effort to become consistent in our performance. And this consistency manifests itself in two distinct ways. Good habits will be consistent with our governing values. That is why they are good. And if I am a person of character, then my good habits must not vary when external circumstances change, no matter how uncomfortable those circumstances may be. Let me illustrate.

The Reverend

My number one governing value is: "I love God with all my heart, mind, and strength." One way I show that love is by praying to God. Now, my governing value insists that I should make prayer a good habit. And my sense of character tells me that that habit should not change just because my external circumstances change. It so happens that my habit has always been to kneel down when I pray, usually at the side of my bed. And I've found it to be a good habit. Perhaps the most difficult test of that habit came when I arrived at Fort Polk, Louisiana, to receive my basic training.

In case you haven't had that wonderful experience, during basic training, the military takes a bright, vibrant young American mind and, in eight weeks, reduces it to an undulating blob of green protoplasm. When I arrived, they took all my hair away, gave me a green suit and a rifle, and said they were going to teach me to kill people.

Because the Vietnam War was picking up momentum, there were lots of people going through basic training. The barracks were overcrowded. I don't know if you've ever seen a military barracks before. It has a roof, four walls, and two stories. Forty young men are normally put on each floor; but because of the war, we had sixty. There were double-deck bunks down both sides of the barracks. These bunks were about two to three feet apart. When I went to bed, I had to sort of slip in sideways and shimmy into bed. There was a wide center corridor with footlockers lined up and down both sides.

I was assigned to the top bunk at the far right-hand corner of the room. At 10:30 that first night I was feeling a little humiliated—no hair and this green suit and everything. As I was about to climb into bed, it dawned on me that it was time for Hyrum Smith to say his prayers. I looked around and there wasn't anybody else praying. I stood there for probably twelve minutes wrestling with myself over all the reasons why it would be okay for me to leap into bed and say one on my back.

I said to myself, "Surely the Lord wouldn't mind. After all, it's really difficult to kneel from the top bunk. I think He would understand that."

I went through this whole rationalization process, but finally I guess I sensed that there was something more at stake there than the question of whether or not God cared where or in which position I prayed. I suppose I understood in a way that giving in to external circumstances was a sign of weak character. So I took a deep breath, bent down, and tapped the fellow who slept underneath me on the shoulder. He had already gone to bed, and he looked at me as if I was from another planet when I said, "Would you mind if I used your bunk to say my prayers?"

Maybe because he was too shocked to think of anything else, he simply said, "Okay." Then he got up and left. I never understood why he had to leave, but he didn't want to be there while I was praying. I knelt down and said my prayers. I don't remember what I prayed about, but I do remember a very uneasy silence for about a two-bed radius. I could feel the fingers pointing at me and imagined such comments as, "What's he doing?"

It got a little easier the next night. The morning after that first night I was named the *Reverend*. In fact, I was called Reverend for the rest of my military experience. Each night it got a little easier to pray on my knees. I developed a little ritual with the fellow under me. (You might say he became a part of my good habit.) I would tap him on the shoulder and he would get up and leave. On the fourth night, one of the fellows came up while I was praying and said, "Hey, can I help you find what you're looking for?"

I said, "No thanks. I'm saying my prayers." You should have seen the look on his face. You see, by now, I was in control. He was reacting to my actions.

Many wonderful things came out of that experience, including having one of the biggest and toughest men in the barracks taking it upon himself to make sure the room was quiet each night when the time came for me to pray. But one of the most important lessons I learned was that the right habits can help you get through the tough places—the times when your resolve falters or following through with a commitment is inconvenient.

Keeping commitments, then, is a matter of character, of will power. Through the pages of this book I can teach you some key natural laws that govern *how* to gain control of your life. I can give you the necessary tools. But I can't give you the strength of will to use them. You have to find that within yourself. What I can do, however, is give you a promise. If you'll try these ideas for twenty-one days, if you'll give them a serious chance, I promise you a major reduction in stress. Why? Ask any medical doctor. Doctors will tell you the best medicine for stress is feeling that you're in control. If you try these ideas—that means identifying your governing values, setting goals, and making and acting on a prioritized task list each day—you'll start feeling the effects of exerting greater control over the events in your life. You'll be more productive and you'll feel better about yourself. With those reinforcements coming your way, you'll find it a lot easier to continue this commitment. And, because your daily actions are actually reflecting your most deeply held values, you will experience an increased measure of inner peace.

PART II

Managing Your Life

By now I hope you feel like you're making some progress along the road to inner peace. If you've been following the suggested exercises I outlined in Part I, you've identified some of your governing values—those things in your life that are of highest priority. You understand the importance of making sure that those governing values are reflected in your daily activities. You have defined one or more long-range goal(s) that will help you do something about one of your governing values, and you have identified some specific intermediate goals that can find their way to your daily task list. And, you have committed yourself to regular daily planning, using a day-planning tool that will help you organize your values, goals, tasks, appointments, and other information related to the events of your life.

So, do you have all you need—all the principles and processes necessary to find inner peace? In a way, yes. If you will follow the system outlined to this point, I can promise that you'll gain greater control of your time and your life and will, as a result, begin to experience greater inner peace as well.

But there are deeper issues at work here as well, and they are the thrust of what we'll discuss in Part II of this book. My discussion of governing values in Law 2 admittedly was a bit streamlined—so that I could lay a simple, straightforward foundation for the Productivity Pyramid. But identifying your personal governing values is a far cry from understanding the complex relationship these values have to specific, day-to-day behavior. For instance, why do people who have the most marvelous values sometimes behave in ways that range from obnoxious to malicious? What is the exact connection between values and behavior? We've talked about how building the Productivity Pyramid can connect your daily activities with your core values. But why do we have to artificially construct that connection? Why don't our values automatically guide us in the things we do from day to day? In other words, why is a Productivity Pyramid even necessary?

As with many things in life, it sometimes helps to gain a second viewpoint of the terrain. In the days before aerial photography, a surveyor always needed to make observations and take bearings from at least two separate points in order to get a precise fix on the location of a distant landmark. In a similar manner, we will look at our objective—finding inner peace—from a different viewpoint in Part II. The next five natural laws will help us dig deeper inside us than the Productivity Pyramid does, enabling us to better understand why we value what we do, why we do what we do, and how we can change beliefs we have about ourselves that are hindering us in our quest for productivity and inner peace.

I'll introduce you to a powerful behavior change tool—the Reality Model—and you'll have a chance to run some of your own beliefs and behavior through the model. In the end, I'll show you how the two models—the Reality Model and the Productivity Pyramid—work together as powerful tools in your quest for inner peace. Then we'll look back over the things we've talked about and I'll try to put them into a broader perspective.

LAW 6

Your behavior is a reflection
of what you *truly* believe

Up until 1988, our basic products at the Franklin Quest Company were time management seminars and the Franklin Day Planner. We had watched the impact that our message was having in the lives of our customers. Productivity had increased, often dramatically. Many individuals were writing to tell us of significant and measurable change in their lives. Managers were reporting improved productivity and positive cultural changes in their organizations. The natural laws and the processes we were teaching were producing more than just an entertaining seminar experience—they were working in people's lives long after the initial training.

At that time, we were teaching ten thousand people a month in live seminars and seeing tremendous changes taking place in their lives. In addition to the things they were learning in the seminar, we wanted to know what was happening inside these people to produce these changes. After all, successful life management often involves change. And so Franklin Quest began a serious inquiry into the mechanics of permanent behavioral change. Our efforts resulted in what we call the Franklin Reality

Model, a simple but powerful tool for understanding motivations and behavior. We now teach this model in many of our advanced seminars.

Simply put, the Franklin Reality Model offers a visual picture of why you behave the way you do. Its greatest value comes from helping you see the clear connection between your beliefs and your behavior. Once I started teaching the model to people, I found it to be a very powerful tool in helping them make better decisions and change behavior for the right reasons. I have discovered that behavior never changes until it is in the self-interest of the person involved to change his or her behavior. Perhaps this model will help you see how change can benefit you.

Here's how the model looks with its different parts. Don't worry if it doesn't make sense to you yet. We'll take a look at the different parts, and then later we'll come back and see how the Reality Model functions.

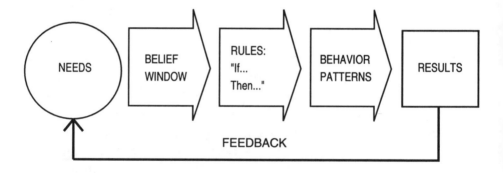

First Element: Needs

If we wanted to talk in purely physical terms, we would say that the only needs people really have are for air, water, food, and shelter from the elements. Psychologists, however, have long maintained that we have psychological wants that are so powerful that they are essential. These psychological needs are constantly impelling us to action of one sort or another. Practically everything we undertake is in response to one or more of these needs. Several lists of basic human needs have been drawn up, but the one I like comes from Dr. Murray Banks, a psychiatrist whose views were popular in the 1950s. He says that four of our basic psychological needs are:

1. The need to **live**
2. The need to **love and be loved**
3. The need to **feel important**
4. The need to experience **variety**.

The Need to Live

No one will dispute the innate need to live. It can be seen in the elderly who struggle against the unyielding pull of death despite physical hardship. It can also be seen in the newly born, who sometimes overcome incredible obstacles to remain alive.

A few years ago a friend of mine had a son born three months premature. The baby weighed just two pounds, ten ounces. And because of severely underdeveloped lungs his chances for survival were not high. Some would claim that medical science worked a miracle in preserving the baby's life, but all the technology in the world would have been useless without what my friend calls "the incredible will to live" that he witnessed in his tiny son. In spite of chronic lung disease and a host of other problems, this little baby struggled on and on for months, never giving in. At one point, after this "preemie" had finally been weaned from the ventilator, the doctors informed my friend that his son was burning off the adult equivalent of eight thousand calories a day just breathing. It would have been so much easier to just stop struggling and give in to the relentless pull of death, but something inside him refused to die. This critically ill baby simply outlasted his medical problems and is now a healthy, rambunctious three-year-old.

This need to live, more intense in some than in others, nonetheless exists in all of us. We desire to live, and this desire is more than simply a conscious choice or a fear of death. It is an incredibly strong natural instinct—so powerful, in fact, that if we feel our lives are in danger we will do many things that we would otherwise not even consider.

We also want to feel safe and secure. That is a manifestation of our desire to live. When we feel safe, the desire to live manifests itself in our search for a stable job, efforts to maintain good health, regular exercise, or even sound investments.

The Need to Love and Be Loved

We read about orphaned infants who simply languish and maybe even die if they are not taken from their cribs and held each day. To love and be loved are more than just desires. They are perhaps the most influential needs we have—even more powerful than the need to live. Consider that most people would willingly put their own lives in great danger or even die to save a loved one, as we have already seen when we talked about crossing the I beam.

There are few scourges as devastating as loneliness, the sense of being abandoned with no one to love or to be loved by. Some people even commit suicide because they are convinced that no one loves them. Their loneliness and lack of sustaining relationships is more unbearable than the thought of ending it all.

We go to great lengths to win love. We join groups that don't really interest us, because they give us a sense of belonging. We associate with people who do things that are not really in our best interest; we put up with behavior that we don't like; we make incredible sacrifices as husbands and wives and friends—because of our desire for love.

Love, as the cliché goes, makes the world go around. Without it life is bland, even unbearable. With it, we find meaning in practically everything we see or do. Love is the greatest motivating force in the world. It gives purpose to everything from working and supporting a family to overcoming addictive behaviors. It is a powerful force—in short, a need.

The Need to Feel Important

"Hey, Daddy, Mommy! Look at me!"

From our earliest years, when we first become aware of ourselves as separate, unique human beings, we have an innate need to feel important, to have others pay attention to us. And as we grow older we seek to enhance those feelings of uniqueness. We do all sorts of things—some significant, some obnoxious—to get people to notice and value us. And if we cannot win their love, we at least want to hold their respect.

Some people have such an overwhelming need to feel important that it propels them to all sorts of extreme behavior. For example, Saddam Hussein put his nation at risk in part to satisfy his need to feel important. Adolf Hitler had an insatiable craving for power. The actions of murderers and thieves often seem to be nothing more than a desperate plea: "Look at me! I did this!" In many cases they leave such obvious clues to follow that investigators conclude that these people actually *want* to be caught. They want people to know what they've done. In a much more innocuous way, people who do absurd things to get their name in the *Guinness Book of World Records* are saying the same thing: "Look at me! I did it!"

Children are open and honest in showing their need to feel important. After performing well at a piano recital or a basketball game or bringing home good grades from school, they look eagerly, expectantly at their family and friends. And they are so genuine in their need for praise that we adults cannot resist giving it.

We all need to feel important, and adults possess this need at least as deeply as children do. And yet as adults we have constructed cultural barriers to seeking praise. It's not okay to feel important, at least not openly. We long to shout, "Look at me! I did well! I'm important!" But such behavior is seen as egotistical. So to fill this need we often resort to less genuine, more stressful means of attracting others' attention, such as trying to take sole credit for something others helped us with.

The Need to Experience Variety

Without variety our lives would be unbearable. For this reason we don't all dress the same—in fact, most people don't wear the same clothes two days in a row. We eat a diversity of foods. (Can you imagine how dreadful it would be to eat even your favorite meal day after day after day?) We read new books, watch new movies, make new friends, buy new music, take vacations to new and exotic places, and go to ball games, concerts, and plays for the sake of infusing a little variety into our lives. We do not grow without variety. If we were to repeat the same experiences and receive the same sensory inputs day after day, we would cease being fully human.

Variety, in fact, is such a compelling need that we sometimes seek it at the expense of the other three needs. We jeopardize our safety, even our lives, for the thrill of skydiving, motorbike racing, rock climbing, hang gliding, bungee jumping, or even more dangerous pursuits. We put relationships at risk when we insist on pursuing new experiences that may injure or offend family members or friends. And we sometimes lose both respect and our own feelings of respectability by seeking variety through behaviors that are considered socially or legally taboo.

Life, love, self-esteem, and variety—these four basic needs lie at the heart of everything we do. Much of human behavior can be explained in terms of our trying to satisfy one or more of these needs.

The Needs Wheel

The four needs can be depicted as quadrants in a circle or wheel, because when all of them are being met, our lives move forward smoothly, like a wheel rolling down the road.

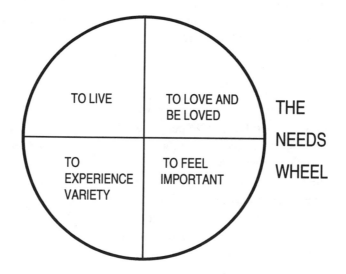

Unfortunately, all four needs are seldom completely satisfied at any given time. When a basic need demands attention, the wheel goes flat, and stops. When this happens, we begin to channel all of our available energy and attention into the need that is being deprived in an effort to make the wheel round again.

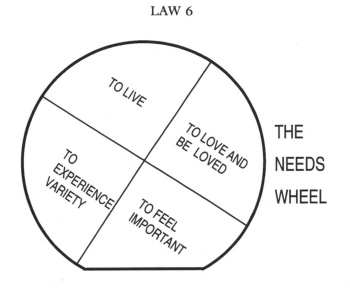

My friends who had the premature baby essentially put their own lives on hold for more than a year, because of the urgent need to give love and care to this sick infant. They sacrificed their own health, their need for variety, and their need to feel important until their little boy was more than a year old. Only then did their lives return more or less to normal.

For the pathological, of course, the need is never filled—the pit has no bottom. Adolf Hitler's megalomania, his need to feel important and powerful, was so great that nothing would satisfy it. He was not content to be the Führer of Germany—he had to acquire new territory from Czechoslovakia, Poland, Austria, France, and Scandinavia. Then he was not content with these conquests—he had to attempt to conquer Russia, Britain, and the United States.

Second Element: The Belief Window

Our four basic needs drive us. But where? The "needs wheel" has no built-in direction; it can roll wherever it will. Some of us spend our lives aimlessly seeking fulfillment of, first, this need, and then, another need—depending on which side of the needs wheel is having trouble at the moment. At the other end of the scale, many people are intensely driven—toward wealth, power, service, the arts, or in other directions. Why do our basic needs produce such a variety of responses? To find the answer, we need to place the needs wheel in the larger context of the Reality Model.

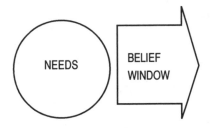

The needs wheel is the first element in the model, because everything starts with our basic needs. Direction, however, or the way we meet those needs, comes from our beliefs. The second element in the Reality Model, then, is what we call the "Belief Window." You, me, and everyone else has a belief window. Your belief window sits, figuratively, in front of your face. Every time you move, that window goes with you. You look at world through that window. You receive information back through that window. On the window is what you believe to be true about the world, yourself, and other people. For example, your experiences or social feedback may have caused you to believe that you are smart, stupid, beautiful, ugly, competent, incompetent, creative, or dull—regardless of whether any of those beliefs is true. And the beliefs on your window exert a powerful influence on your actions and behavior.

Many of the beliefs on your belief window are ones you think will help you meet your basic needs. "Smoking causes lung cancer" is a belief obviously related to our need to live. Somewhat related to the need to live (and also to the need to feel important) is a belief like "Lots of money will solve my problems." A belief like "An expensive new car will improve my image" could be aimed at helping us feel important or be loved.

Your belief window itself is neither good nor bad. It is just there as the receptacle of all these beliefs you have accumulated. On this window you have placed hundreds of things that you believe are correct. The number of beliefs you have on your belief window is a function of your experiences and, therefore, your age. Typically, the older you are, the more beliefs you have.

What's Written on Your Belief Window?

So on your belief window you have placed all the things you *believe to be true* about the patterns you see in the world, yourself, and those around you. They might be as simple and obvious as: "Objects will fall to the ground when dropped from the top of a building." Another example might be: "Antibiotics kill bacteria that cause infections." These are examples of things we believe that are based on a scientific evidence and testing, and thus could be considered as "correct" beliefs—reflecting reality, or things as they *really* are. Such beliefs could also be considered as "natural laws." A belief like "Women are more compassionate than men" may be less absolute, but still generally true, based on wide experience. On the other hand, a belief such as "The world is flat," once widely held by many people, has been proven to be "incorrect" or "untrue." Sometimes our beliefs accurately reflect reality; sometimes they do not. The beliefs on our belief windows may be strongly backed by scientific evidence, while others may be completely subjective on our part. The important thing to remember is that because we *believe* them all to be true, we will *act* as if they are true.

Our Beliefs Can Be Reflections of Our Values

The things we believe in are often reflections of our values. In fact, if we are objective enough to analyze the things we believe, we can often deduce from them some underlying values that we may never have consciously recognized. Let's look at a few examples of beliefs that reflect a whole spectrum of values. Note that most of these deal with topics about which there is no consensus on what is absolute truth:

ABORTION
• An unborn child is a person.
• A woman has the right to choose what happens inside her own body.

MILITARY BUILD-UP
- The Cold War is over. We should greatly reduce military spending.
- A Russian threat still exists. We should leave the military budget where it is.
- The Cold War is over, but there are other threats. We don't need some of our previous military strength, but should maintain a strong but flexible military.

EDUCATION
- Schools should go back to basics.
- Schools are too traditional and should explore new educational methods.

COMPARABLE WORTH
- People should be paid on the basis of their worth as human beings, regardless of the law of supply and demand.
- It is impossible to set wages fairly except by market forces.
- Some people are simply worth more than others.

HOMOSEXUAL RIGHTS
- One's sexual orientation is innate and cannot be changed; homosexuality is like having green eyes.
- Homosexuality is learned behavior.

POLITICS
- The political system is broken. We should scrap it and start over.
- Our system is not perfect, but it's the best one in the world.

BETWEEN THE SEXES
- Men hate women.
- Women should be put in their place.
- A woman's place is in the home.
- Women have as much right as men to positions of influence.
- Men are inferior.

RELIGION
- God will save only those who confess Jesus Christ as Savior.
- God doesn't care what you believe as long as you are a good person.
- There is no God.

MUSIC
- Rock music is satanic.
- Rock music is loud, but morally harmless.
- Rock music is physically harmful.
- Rock music is *not* music.
- Country/western (or classical, or new age, or easy listening, or jazz, or whatever) is the only true music.

FAMILY RELATIONSHIPS
- Mom and Dad will always love me, regardless of what I do.
- My parents (or husband or wife) will never understand me.
- My parents (or husband or wife) made me the way I am.

SELF-ESTEEM
- My worth as a person is determined by:
  —the praise I receive from others
  —the things I own
  —the job I hold
  —the way I look
  —the kind of person I marry
  —any combination of the above
  —none of the above.

RESPONSIBILITY
- I'm a pawn of outside forces and can't do anything about it.
- Everything that goes wrong is my fault.

Obviously this list is not exhaustive. It is only intended to help you recognize that there are many possible beliefs connected to every issue and that there may be alternative beliefs to the ones you have on your belief window. Most of these are reflections of certain underlying values. For instance, the two beliefs, "An unborn child is a person" and "A woman has the right to choose what happens inside her own body," spring from two radically different values, and because these beliefs lead to certain behaviors, there is a terrible conflict going on in our country. Both sides believe they are right, because they judge both their actions and the actions of others in light of their values.

Everyone has correct, incorrect, and debatable beliefs that influence behavior. Remember, in using the terms "correct" and "incorrect," I am not attempting to make moral judgments about whether beliefs are "good" or "bad." If a belief reflects natural law or reality, it may be considered as generally "correct." If it's not rooted in reality and, hence, just doesn't work, it may be considered as "incorrect." A belief may also be a subjective judgment, a matter of opinion, but not clearly provable as either "correct" or "incorrect." In all these cases, though, the key is to identify the beliefs on our window and change those that are incorrect or inadequate.

One thing we don't always realize about beliefs, though, is that we can perform tests—either actively or through observation—to see if they are true, false, or just matters of opinion. Scientists are in the business of testing beliefs (they call them hypotheses or theories), and through their efforts the world has replaced many incorrect beliefs with correct (or at least *more* correct) ones.

By contrast, the problem with our personal beliefs is that we put them on our belief window and consider them as absolutely correct without knowing whether they truly describe reality or are just misconceptions on our part. And this lack of testing on our part can cause trouble for us because, regardless of their degree of soundness, we conduct our lives as if everything written on our window is true.

Sometimes, in addition to a personal belief window, we acquire what might be called a collective belief window. This window is filled with beliefs we pick up in collective settings, like work. When we look through two windows at the same time, we may find that the beliefs on one sometimes conflict with the those on the other, and we have to choose which window to give higher priority to. The culture of the organization where you work, for instance, represents a collective belief window, and on that window you may find a belief that insists on a high degree of conformity among employees. If your own belief window says, "Individuality and creativity are important," then you will have to choose which belief to follow. If you choose to conform, you may find yourself highly frustrated. If, on the other hand, you choose to express your individuality at work, you may be branded a maverick and be overlooked for promotions and raises because you aren't a "good corporate citizen." Or, perhaps, by recognizing these two belief windows and the conflicting things on them, you may choose to find new employment, where the collective window is more in harmony with your personal beliefs.

Third Element: Rules

For each belief on your window, you subconsciously create rules that govern your behavior. These rules are "if-then" statements that translate your beliefs into actions. If you believe, for example, that "All Doberman pinschers are vicious" (a belief clearly related to one of the four basic needs—to live), you immediately start to establish rules that will govern your behavior regarding Dobermans. These rules exist, more often than not, only at a subconscious level, but they do exist.

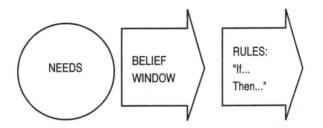

A rule stemming from this belief might look something like this: "If all Doberman pinschers are vicious, then when I see a Doberman walking around unchained, I'll leap tall buildings with a single bound. I'll get away, run, evade. And I'll do the same thing every time." Another rule might be: "If all Doberman pinschers are vicious, then I will never own a Doberman pinscher. I will buy a Saint Bernard or a Pekingese or a poodle or anything else instead."

You should understand that the first three elements of this model—needs, beliefs, and rules—are usually going on inside your mind where nobody can see what's happening, not even you. These rules operate at the subconscious level, so that we are able to act automatically whenever we find ourselves in dangerous situations.

Fourth Element: Behavior Patterns

The fourth piece of the model is called "Behavior Patterns." This is where something physically happens. Consequently, this is the point at which the workings of the model start becoming visible.

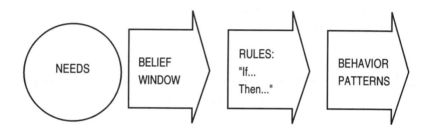

Let's return to the belief, "All Doberman pinschers are vicious." If you walk into my yard with that written on your belief window and I have a Doberman running around loose, what are you going to do? Well, the rule you set up will automatically take charge of your behavior. You will jump the fence, climb a tree, or rush back out and close the gate. Or, if you really need to see me, you may go to your car, retrieve your rifle, and approach the house like a soldier behind enemy lines.

Fifth Element: Results and Feedback

The fifth element in the model is called "Results." This element makes the model an incredibly powerful tool in helping you gain control of your life.

Note that the "Results" box has an arrow representing "Feedback" tying it back to the needs wheel. If the results of your behavior meet your needs, this feedback tells you that you have a correct belief or harmless opinion on your belief window. If your needs are not met, this suggests that you should take a closer look at both your needs and the belief you are using to try to satisfy them. But how do you know whether or not your needs are being met by a certain belief? Well, the only way you can know for sure is to put the behavior to the test of time. *Results often take time to measure.*

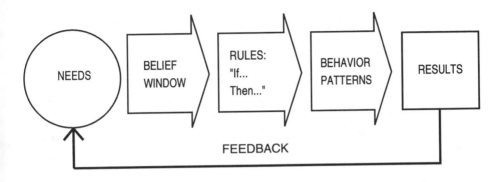

For example, if you spend years and years avoiding Doberman pinschers like the plague, and you never get attacked by one, you may conclude from your own observations that your belief is correct. At least it's true that your need—to stay alive and remain safe—is being met.

Sometimes, though, safety is not our highest priority. Perhaps one of our other needs exerts itself and takes precedence over the need to live. Then we have a conflict. Suppose, for instance, that you have "All Doberman pinschers are vicious" written on your belief window, but that it shares space with another belief: "Macho guys aren't afraid of dogs." What need drives this belief? The need to feel important, obviously. But these two beliefs are in conflict. You can't follow both of them. In this case, you prioritize, subconsciously, and give higher value to one belief over the other. If feeling macho is more important to you than feeling safe, then you may be a bit uneasy around Dobermans, but you won't avoid them. You'll swagger past them, pretending to ignore them. And you may get attacked. That's the price you pay for giving more value to the belief that has the higher priority. And getting attacked may convince you to change a belief. You may erase "Macho guys aren't afraid of Doberman pinschers" from your window and replace it with "Smart guys *are* afraid of Doberman pinschers."

The process of amending our beliefs happens all the time. It's called experience, and it's an important ingredient in successful life management. Ben Franklin wrote, "Experience keeps a dear school, but fools will learn in no other." As another writer put it, "Good judgment comes from experience; experience comes from poor judgment." Our experiences cause us to alter our beliefs, adopt new ones, or give them a higher value.

The Reality Model—a Powerful Tool

To summarize, the two major functions of the Reality Model are these:

First, it gives you a visual picture of what is going on in your life and helps you understand why. This is the function we have been examining in this chapter. Whether you have previously recognized them or not, you do have the four basic needs—the same needs I have. You have placed beliefs on your belief window that you think will help you meet those needs, and you have established some rules, and those rules are governing your behavior. The model also allows you to take a look at the results of your behavior and determine whether or not your beliefs are serving your interest.

The second major function of the model is that it can help you evaluate beliefs *before* they affect your behavior. Used this way, you can predict the types of behavior that may result from a particular belief. Then you can change or modify the belief instead of simply being reactive and allowing it to happen or trying to remedy the problem by going after the behavior. This use of the Reality Model also allows you to evaluate whether or not alternative beliefs would better serve you by helping you see the potential behavior that they would produce. In Law 7 we'll take a closer look at this second function of the Reality Model and how we can use it to change behaviors that are not meeting our needs.

In addition to these two primary ways the Reality Model can help us better understand ourselves, it also helps us understand someone else's behavior and the possible beliefs driving it. When you observe a pattern of behavior you can tell quite a bit about what is on a person's belief window. Conversely, if you know what is on a person's belief window you can predict with some accuracy their behavior, and ultimately, the results of that behavior. This makes the model an even more powerful tool.

For example, could the world have known what was on Adolf Hitler's belief window? The fact is that, yes, we could have. How? Hitler wrote a book—*Mein Kampf (My Struggle)*. In it he told us what was on his belief window in considerable detail. For example, one of the beliefs on his window, as revealed by *Mein Kampf*, was that the races were graded. There were, according to him, superior races and inferior races. The highest race, according to Adolf Hitler, was the Aryan race—the race destined to be masters. The lowest races were the Jews and blacks—those who, in Hitler's view, were the root of all of civilization's evils and ills.

Could we predict Hitler's behavior by knowing that he had this belief on his belief window? Again, yes, we could. In fact, some people did. The predictions were so ugly that for a long time no one would believe them. In the genocide that Hitler perpetrated during World War II, millions of people died—as a result of a messed-up belief window. Now, did the results of Hitler's behavior meet his (or his country's) needs over time? How long did Hitler's predicted thousand-year Reich last? Only twelve years. Adolf Hitler died in its ashes.

The model can be a powerful tool in studying and evaluating history, and even more exciting, in researching historical figures. For example, you can ask yourself the question, "What was on Abraham Lincoln's belief window?" Can we tell by what he did, by his behavior patterns, what was there? I think we could have quite an interesting time discovering that. What was on the belief window of Joan of Arc? Florence Nightingale? Theodore Roosevelt? Winston Churchill? Martin Luther King? Margaret Thatcher? Saddam Hussein? Mikhail Gorbachev? Their behavior had significant impact on the history of their nations or the world at large. What each had written on his or her belief window prompted that behavior. Can we, by studying what they did, go back and find out what they believed? I'd like to suggest that we can. Had others at the time been able to read their belief windows would it have changed history? Would events have turned out differently—for better or worse? Possibly.

Stated Beliefs vs. Actual Beliefs

The Reality Model helps us to see the clear connection between our beliefs and our behavior. But what about those things we *think* we really believe, but never actually do anything about? Or what about all the things we believe we shouldn't do, but do anyway? I don't pretend to be a psychologist, and all the complexities of human motivations and behavior cannot be understood through a tool like the Reality Model. But it can help us understand the general patterns of why we do (or don't do) what we think we should or should not do.

Sometimes our "beliefs" may actually be things we only *think* we believe because of duty or the expectations of others. My colleague Jerry Pulsipher graduated from high school and entered college at the time when the Soviet Union had just placed the first artificial satellite, *Sputnik*, into orbit, beating the United States in the opening chapter of the space race. The patriotic outcry at the time called for more engineers and scientists, and Jerry believed that he should major in one of the sciences. He already had an interest in geology, a science that would have great import in future explorations of the moon and other planets. As he entered the university that fall, Jerry really believed that he could and should become a geologist.

But two quarters later, in spite of having been an honor student in high school and spending many sleepless nights studying, Jerry was failing in college chemistry and math, two of the essential subjects needed to become a geologist. Rather than beat his head against the wall for another term, he looked at what was written on his belief window. Despite his earlier belief that he *should* be a geologist, when he looked down deep he realized he really didn't believe that at all. And because he didn't believe it, it wasn't happening. What he really loved was writing and art and music, and Jerry made the decision to major in journalism, with a healthy dose of the fine arts on the side. That experience changed his grades from D's to A's, and, more importantly, moved him toward some significant contributions later in his life that grew naturally out of his immersion in writing and art. When his behavior reflected what he *really* believed about himself and what he should be doing, he began to meet his needs and experience inner peace.

All of us have had instances where we thought we believed something to be true, but in fact were doing nothing about it. Take weight loss or physical fitness, for example. How many of us believe intellectually that we should lose some pounds or be more physically active? We've read all about the strong medical connections between weight and fitness, and illnesses like heart disease or stroke. Then why don't we reflect that belief in our behavior and lose the weight or shape up? If believing that something is true actually directs our behavior, why doesn't our behavior change once we've bought the new belief?

If I had the complete answer to that question, I could solve a lot of human ills. But viewed in the context of the Reality Model, what often happens in such cases is that we have another belief at work that is overriding or negating the belief we consciously know is true. For example, a person who "knows" he or she should lose weight or stop smoking or get more physically fit may also have the hidden and unstated belief that "It (heart disease, lung cancer, stroke, etc.) won't happen to me. I'll beat the odds." Of course, that is not a correct belief—it doesn't reflect reality—and such a belief will certainly not meet our needs in the end. But in the meantime, its hold on us may be powerful enough to override another belief we consciously know to be true. If we can remove the deep-seated incorrect belief, then our behavior would start to come in line with the correct belief.

The important thing to remember is that, in general, our behavior does in fact reflect what we *really* believe, and if our behavior doesn't seem to be reflecting a consciously stated belief, we should take a careful look at conflicting beliefs on our window.

Inadequate Beliefs

Sometimes our needs go unmet, not because we are following incorrect beliefs—perhaps our beliefs are correct—but because our belief windows contain significant blind spots. Perhaps we aren't even aware of certain possible beliefs that may lead to the results we're after, because we haven't learned about them yet. Let me illustrate.

My friend and former colleague Senator Bob Bennett tells a story about Bob Mullen, founder of a Washington-based PR firm who began his career as a reporter back in the 1930s. One of Mullen's first newspapers was in Denver, and on his lunch hour one day, as he was walking through a section of town that was unfamiliar to him, he saw a sign on a storefront that said: THE GREAT CANADIAN GRAY GOOSE FLYING MACHINE COMPANY. He was intrigued by the name and dropped into a lecture given by the company's president who said he was there to tell them about his product. First, however, they needed to understand the premise on which the company was built; namely, that God is the Greatest Engineer of All. Given that fact, the president (we'll call him Fred) suggested, then it only makes sense that God's creations will be better engineered than man's. Hence, if we wish to build an airplane (or flying machine), we should follow God's pattern in our planning. This was exactly what the company had done, using as its model the finest of all God's flyers—the Great Canadian Gray Goose.

Fred had studied the Great Canadian Gray Goose carefully and was certain he had discovered the secret of its unparalleled flying ability. "When the wings are raised, the feathers are turned and spread like my fingers, so that the air can pass through. The wings rise without hindrance through the air. On the downward beat, however, the feathers turn to close off all passage of air so that the wing can beat a powerful lifting stroke. That's the secret, the secret of the Great Canadian Gray Goose, and I am going to build a flying machine that is based on that secret."

Then came the inevitable sales pitch. "I want you to help me," Fred said. "I need money to make this machine a reality. I want you to buy shares in my company and help me build a flying machine based on the principles of the Greatest Aeronautical Engineer of All." Then he passed the plate up and down the aisles. (This has to be the strangest stock offering I've ever heard of.) A number of people gave him ten dollars for a share in the company.

When the new shareholders had vacated the store, Mullen approached the president of The Great Canadian Gray Goose Flying Machine Company. Fred, he learned, was a former minister who had come to Denver for health reasons and hadn't been able to find work. But one day, as he pondered the beauty of the birds and God's other creations, the idea of The Great Canadian Gray Goose Flying Machine came to him. He had chosen this unusual way to raise money, he said, "because it is the only way I know."

The young reporter went back to the office to write the story, and followed the company's progress after that. He was present at Denver's Stapleton Airport when The Great Canadian Gray Goose Flying Machine, complete with movable wings and little air holes that were open on the upstroke but closed on the down, collapsed during its first attempted takeoff. And he sadly chronicled Fred's later indictment on charges of stock fraud.

What do you suppose was on Fred's belief window? If you had approached Fred with the notion that he had a belief window and asked him to identify what was written on his window, I suppose he would have told you something like this: "I believe in God. I believe in working hard. I believe in being fair and hurting no one. I believe in full disclosure of my intentions." He may or may not have added: "If I hold to these basics, I am sure to win out in the end."

But he didn't win out in the end. Instead, he found himself penniless, humiliated, and in serious legal trouble. Which of his beliefs led him astray? The answer, of course, is none of them. There were, however, other factors at work that he had ignored—the laws of aerodynamics, for instance. Whether you believe in God or evolution as the creator of the Great Canadian Gray Goose, the fact is that the bird flies in accordance with the laws of aerodynamics, and Fred knew virtually none of them. It is not the way the goose flaps its wings that is crucial—it can fly with its wings held motionless. It's the airfoil *shape* of the wing (along with many other factors) that matters. Ignorant of all this, Fred could be absolutely sincere in his beliefs and he could work hard and be as honest as possible and still fail to get off the ground.

Now, we may not be planning to build a flying machine, but we all make the same kind of mistakes Fred made: In essence, we commit ourselves to a set of beliefs and then forge ahead, thinking we will succeed at whatever it is we are attempting. "How can I possibly fail?" we reason. "My beliefs are perfectly sound." But we do fail, and in analyzing our failure, we conclude that there were other factors involved, other factors we had totally disregarded.

This represents a substantial part of the growing, learning experience that life should be. We must constantly discover and add better, more correct beliefs to our belief windows and figure out how they function in concert with the beliefs we already possess. Otherwise we will not gain control over our lives.

We can learn from Fred's "missing" beliefs. We can also learn from the one incorrect belief Fred had on his belief window. Fred apparently believed that trust in God, good intentions, and hard work were enough to enable him to succeed at anything. Although all those attributes are commendable, they are not enough to justify our disregard of other pertinent factors we must understand. We must not only remain open to new information, we must actively seek it out and try to gain a more complete understanding of the world as it really is.

Now that you've been introduced to the Reality Model, it's a good time to go back and look again at some of the governing values you identified earlier in Part I. Ask yourself if they are reflected in or affected by any of the things you have written on your belief window. Because it's so difficult to see what's on your own belief window, you may wish to seek the help of a spouse or trusted friend. Someone who knows you well can see things on your belief window that are not apparent to you because you have never questioned their validity.

Your list of governing values will suggest some beliefs already on your belief window. If marital or family relationships are important to you, you'll probably see beliefs like "Relationships between a husband and wife should be based on mutual respect," or "When individuals bring different talents and viewpoints to the table, the marriage (or family) is stronger. The whole is more than the sum of its parts."

At the same time, you may find some beliefs that will surprise you: "Because my spouse doesn't think like I do, I must dominate in the relationship," or "My way is always the best way." Regardless of the beliefs you identify, the important thing is to examine what's written on *your* belief window. Only when you know what's there can you begin to do something about it. How we change incorrect or less than satisfactory beliefs is what we'll discuss in Law 7.

LAW 7

You satisfy needs when your beliefs are in line with reality

How can you tell whether a belief, attitude, or opinion on your belief window is correct? The fifth element in our Reality Model gives us a clue. If the *results* of your behavior meet one or more of your four basic needs, you probably have a correct belief. Conversely, if the results do not meet your needs, you can be fairly sure the belief in question is incorrect.

Let's put this to the test. Let's say you're late for an appointment and hurrying to get there. If you believe that "A competent driver like me can safely drive above the speed limit" and you do indeed drive that fast at times, and you're still alive, does this mean this belief is correct? Well, not necessarily. You see, *results often take time to measure.* If we touch something hot, we will know the results immediately. But the results of many other actions may take years to become evident.

But what if you have followed that belief your whole life and have never had an accident, never even gotten a ticket? Is it a correct belief? Again, not necessarily. Sometimes, when we're operating on an incorrect assumption, we manage to beat the odds. Sometimes we're lucky. For this reason, it's often wise to perform two tests on some of our beliefs—

one through our own experiences, one through the experiences of others. In this particular case, we could look at data regarding fast drivers— perhaps statistics about the average speed of drivers involved in traffic accidents, or drivers who ended up as traffic fatalities. Perhaps statistics about the frequency of accidents for both speeders and nonspeeders would be relevant. Or maybe we could consider the potential impact of driving eighty-five miles per hour on such things as driving records and insurance premiums. Sometimes common sense or potential bad results are enough to cause us to look for better beliefs. "Safety is more important than punctuality" might be a more reasonable alternative.

The idea that "the speed laws don't apply to me" also suggests other beliefs at work. One of these may be, "It's okay to leave late for appointments." "Being late for appointments is bad for business" might be another. Perhaps changing one of these other beliefs will make the speeding belief irrelevant. "Arriving late for an appointment isn't the end of the world" would be an example. Or perhaps, "Leaving early for appointments is a must." Another might be, "Not breaking the law is very important to me." Any of these belief window assumptions would eliminate the perceived need to rationalize excessive speeding.

Let's look at another belief: "My self-worth is dependent on never losing an argument." Do you know anyone who has this written on his or her belief window? Which of the four needs would drive a belief like that? The need to feel important, definitely. Sometimes the need to be loved gets mixed up in it. Now let's take it through the model.

If you assume this belief is true, then you set up some subconscious rules that govern your behavior. What if you get in an argument with your ten-year-old son? What do you do? *Even if you know your son is right, what do you do?* Poor kid. The most important question, though, is this: Do the results of this behavior satisfy your needs in the long term? In the short term maybe your ego gets a boost. Maybe you feel important. You've reasserted your authority or domination over your son, but in the long term, even in the short term, how's he going to feel about you? Right. He'd trade you in on a new model without blinking an eye. The results of your behavior may temporarily satisfy your need to feel important, but it certainly doesn't satisfy other needs, such as the need to love and be loved. The idea that you must never lose an argument is, therefore, an incorrect belief.

Changing Circumstances Can Reveal
Incorrect Beliefs

Robert F. Bennett, in his book *Gaining Control: Your Key to Freedom &
Success*, uses an example that illustrates an important point about incorrect
beliefs. A wife (let's call her Rhoda) worked with her husband (Ronald)
all during the early struggling years of their marriage. As he went through
school and in early entrepreneurial efforts, she was heavily involved in his
affairs. Being bright and well educated herself, she was a tremendous
help to him. "They are a great team," people would say. "One of the
advantages of working with him is that you get her thrown in as part of
the deal." Some of their happiest years as a married couple were the years
of financial struggle. Their model looked like this:

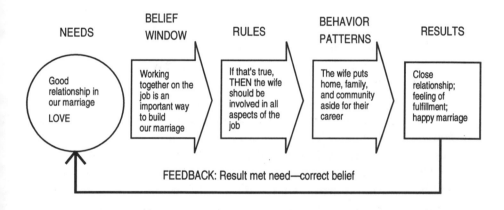

Then the hard work paid off—he joined a large firm that, impressed with
his "self-starter" pattern of success, posted him to a new office in an Asian
country where executives' wives were not expected to be involved in their
husbands' activities, except on a social level. As the business boomed, he
spent more and more time at the office; she spent more and more time alone.
There were no children in the house—they "hadn't had time" because of
their working together in the early years. When he became the head of the
office, he was away even more. Since it was not considered proper for Rhoda
to do anything but sit at home and revel in her new affluence, she became

truly bored. Before long, she had a drinking problem, and then there was a divorce.

Looking at this situation from the perspective of the Reality Model, we might conclude that Rhoda and Ronald originally had a belief about their relationship that was based in reality, but the more restrictive foreign culture did not allow them to implement that belief—that's why the marriage failed. That's only partially true, though. There were also some incorrect beliefs, hidden in their "true" one, which the new context brought to light.

Ronald bought the questionable belief that his marriage was based primarily on its financial stability; he ignored all Rhoda's other needs, assuming as many people do that wealth and status are ends in themselves rather than means to other ends.

Rhoda bought the incorrect belief that being cut out of her husband's business life had deprived her of the only meaningful thing she could do. When circumstances changed (which, by the way, they always do), she no longer felt important. This fundamental need wasn't being met. Perhaps she even felt less love, felt that Ronald was ignoring her. To meet those needs she added new beliefs to her window. Perhaps one of them was, "Drinking makes me feel better." Another may have been, "My unhappiness is all Ronald's fault, because he ignores me and doesn't spend any time with me." These beliefs then led to drinking and divorce. And the results of these behaviors weren't going to meet her frustrated needs. She had fallen into the vicious circle we talked about in the previous section.

Suppose, however, that Ronald had said to himself, "Rhoda's sense of self-worth is just as important to our marriage as money"—a new belief. It would have led him to ask, "How can I help her maintain her self-esteem now that she can't come to the office anymore?" His actions would have been different.

And suppose Rhoda had said to herself, "Well, I'm faced with a new situation, but I'm still in control of how I will react"—a true statement. That would have led her to say, "I don't need the old supports, nice as they were; I'll find new ones," and alcohol would not have been so attractive to her.

Sometimes an incorrect belief will work for us temporarily—until circumstances change. Then suddenly our needs are not being met. This serves as warning to us that our beliefs sometimes need to be revised to reflect changing circumstances. The point is that *we have control over what we choose to believe.*

We can examine our belief window and either replace or rearrange what's written on it at any time.

Growth Means Change

Personal growth, you might say, is the process of improving what is on your belief window. The first step is accepting the possibility that some of the things on your window are wrong. The willingness to do this is a sign of maturity.

After I finished presenting a seminar to one of our major clients, a working mother, one of the company's fine human resource executives, approached me. She described the transformation that had taken place in her mind as we were discussing the whole subject of correct and incorrect beliefs. She told me about the belief she had been living with for a long time: "Good moms stay at home." Then she described the guilt feelings she had been dealing with on a daily basis and how this affected her performance as both an executive and a mother.

Her belief was obviously incorrect, and she had realized this during the presentation. What about single mothers or mothers in two-income families who simply have to work to provide food, shelter, and clothing for their children? Are they "bad" mothers because they work? Of course not. There is no connection between "good mothers" and staying at home. You can work and be a good mother. Through the seminar this particular woman began to understand that her assumption that "Good moms stay at home" was yielding very unsatisfactory results in her life and she reevaluated it. Then she told me the new belief she was replacing the old one with. It went like this: "Good moms are there when their children need them." This new belief gave her the peace of mind to increase her effectiveness at work and to focus her attention on the needs of her children.

We have kept in touch after that time. She became a better employee and a better mother. Instead of spending her energy on guilt feelings and self-fulfilling prophecies, she was able to focus it creatively on more important matters.

The Puppet and the Puppeteer

Bob Bennett used to tell the story about a friend of his (we'll call him Sam) whose father was a very domineering man. As we might expect from such an individual, he wanted to mold Sam in his own image, force him to have the same values, and make him walk down the same career path that he had. Sam, as we also might expect, rebelled against this pressure and deliberately did the opposite of what his father wanted. As soon as he was old enough, he left home to get away from his father, hoping that his resentment against the man would finally fade away. It didn't. In fact, it continued to grow as the years passed. Sam never felt free of his father's attempts to control him and wanted desperately to do something about it.

Finally, Sam decided to face the music and "have things out" with his father once and for all. He knew the old man was strong-willed and that the confrontation would be a nasty affair for his mother, with whom he had a loving relationship. Still, he felt compelled to get it off his chest, regardless of the consequences. It would be "good" for him psychologically, he reasoned. This was a basic belief that had been taking shape on his belief window.

So he set out in his car for the small rural community where his parents lived. On the way, though, Sam thought it all through again and came to the realization for the first time in his life that he had been acting like a puppet all these years, responding to his father's pull on the strings with the exact opposite movement from the one the old man expected. The surprising revelation that came to him, however, was that *he* and not his father had been the one who had kept the strings attached.

Sam realized that the strings connecting him to his father were the beliefs he had written on his window that he must always oppose his father's wishes and do exactly the opposite of what his father wanted him to do. With dismay, he had to acknowledge that for many years he had reacted to his father according to those beliefs. The fact that he had been unhappy and frustrated over their relationship all these years told him that the beliefs were incorrect.

He came to the conclusion that there were basically three ways he could deal with his father. He could rebel, which he had been doing now for years. When he was growing up, if his dad said to be in at ten o'clock, he would stay out until twelve, even if he didn't want to. And this behavior continued, even after he had left home. By rebelling, though,

Sam was not cutting the strings as he had hoped to; he was simply switching the hand and foot strings. His dad would pull what he thought was a hand string, and Sam's foot would move. The puppeteer didn't get the response he wanted, and that would frustrate him, but he was still the one who was controlling the puppet's actions. In other words, Sam didn't stay out until midnight because he wanted to, but *because* his dad wanted him in by ten.

The second possible reaction was for Sam to try to become the puppeteer. He could think, I'll slip from Dad's control by controlling *him*. He knew just what would make his father furious, and he could make him dance by pulling on all the right strings. Many teenagers do this. They know just which profanities to use, how loud to play their music, which friends to bring home, what clothes to wear, and so on. But a puppeteer is still dependent on the strings for his act to work. Neither the puppet nor the puppeteer is free. And any human relationship based on manipulation is headed for trouble. Sam knew that happiness couldn't be based on his ability or inability to manipulate his father. So, becoming the puppeteer was not the answer.

The third possibility, and the only promising one, was for Sam to simply cut the strings. He could act instead of react. Then he would be free to be himself—not the person his father wanted him to be, but also not the exact opposite of what his father wanted. The minute he came to the realization that *he controlled how he would live his life*, the strings simply fell away.

By the time he reached his parents' home, he felt that no confrontation was necessary. So he walked into the house, went to his father, and told him he loved him, visited with both his father and mother for a few minutes, and then drove home—minus the heavy load he had been carrying for years. When he finally shed the belief, "I must rebel against everything my father wants," he was instantly happier, a good sign that he had erased an incorrect belief and replaced it with a better one.

Five Rules for Changing What's Written on Your Belief Window

I'd like to share with you five basic rules, a five-step formula, for gaining control of your life. The formula is based on the concept of cognitive dissonance, in which psychologists tell us that our minds cannot hold two conflicting viewpoints at the same time, we will automatically seek to resolve the conflict by choosing the more logical viewpoint and rejecting the other. The formula looks like this:

1. *Identify the behavior pattern that is not producing the desired results.*
2. *Identify possible beliefs driving the behavior.*
3. *Predict future behavior based on following those beliefs.*
4. *Identify alternative beliefs that may produce better results.*
5. *Predict future behavior based on the new beliefs.*

Let me illustrate this process with a story from my own family. I have a son named Joseph. When he was in high school he took second place in a Tom Cruise look-alike contest. Ugly kid. He also made the high school basketball team. He was very excited about it. But I watched his behavior. At the first of the season I went to a couple of his games, and I noticed that whenever he'd shoot the ball and miss, he'd never shoot again. If he ran into somebody on the floor, had body contact, he'd back away and stop being aggressive. He exhibited similar behavior off the basketball court. If he got a bad grade in school, for instance, he was just ugly to be around. He hated to bring bad grades home.

So I sat down with him on a Sunday morning and said, "Joseph, I've been watching some of your behavior. Can I describe some of this behavior in an effort to find some things on your belief window?" Now, there was no threat here, because we were talking about the belief window, and he understands the Reality Model very well. He understands that I still love him as an individual even if I tell him his belief window is screwed up, because he is separate from his belief window. The wonderful thing we need to remember here is that you can be very confrontive about someone's belief window without ever attacking the human being. You are attacking something they can fix. In other words, "I'm okay, Dad, right?" "Yeah, you're okay. I love you a lot. Your belief window needs surgery, but you're okay."

Because Joseph understood this, I was able to describe his behavior to him. "Whenever you shoot and miss, you never shoot again. When you run into somebody, you back away and stop being aggressive. When you get a bad grade in school, you're ugly to be around. You don't like to bring bad grades home. Now, that's the behavior. Why do you behave that way? Do you think we can identify some things that might be on your belief window driving that behavior?" When you get to Step 2 in this process, you have to start asking the question, "Why?" Why are you behaving this way? The response to that question comes back in the form of a belief on the window.

We talked about this for twenty-five minutes—it took quite a while—and at the end of that time my son sat back in his chair and said, "Well, you need to understand, Dad, that I'm terribly afraid of failure."

I said, "You know, Joseph, I think we just found one of the assumptions on your belief window. The belief is: 'Failure is bad.' Where did you ever get an idea like that?" And do you know what the answer was? From me!

He got emotional, and he said, "You don't know anything about failure, Dad."

"What do you mean I don't know anything about failure?"

"Yeah, you've never failed. You go all over the world giving talks, everybody thinks you walk on water, you've got all this stuff." (Have you ever noticed how kids always equate success with "stuff"—material possessions?) "You don't know how to spell failure," he added for emphasis. He was very emotional.

Well, I could see he didn't have a clear picture of his dad, so I said, "Let me tell you about my failures." I then spent ninety minutes describing my failures. I have had five major financial disasters. I made the mistake of telling him about my grades in school. I described my failures in detail. And as I did this, Joseph's whole countenance changed. It was like taking a rock off his back.

He sat there kind of stunned and said, "You mean it's okay to fail?"

"Of course it's okay to fail. The only thing wrong with failure is if you don't do anything about it."

It was easy, once we identified the incorrect belief, to predict his behavior if he didn't change what was on his belief window. He would have been afraid to try anything new, afraid to exert his talents, test his limits, and expand his horizons. You might say he would have lived a life of constant failure—simply because he was afraid to fail.

We put a new belief on his window that day: "Failure is part of growth." And we could easily predict the behavior that would result from that belief.

Two days later I went to a basketball game. He was playing against a rival high school, and that kid had turned into an animal. He started shooting when he shouldn't shoot. He started enjoying running over people. He'd bring a bad grade home from school, triumphant. "Hey, ever see anything like that, Dad? Got a D." We had to have a whole new conversation about belief windows and grades. He'd gone a bit too far in the other direction. Instead of believing that failure was bad, he now believed it wasn't just necessary—it was desirable. Well, we got that straightened out, but the wonderful thing about this experience is that the pain, the hurt in his life stopped, when he realized it was okay to make a mistake.

Now, did you follow the steps in that experience? We identified the behavior. We identified a belief. We predicted some future behavior. We came up with a new belief. We predicted some future behavior based on the new belief. He liked the new belief a whole lot more than the old one—and healing started. Behavior started to change for the right reasons.

Let's look at another example. I know a good many people who could be classified as workaholics. Now, I pride myself in working hard—there's nothing wrong with this. But I see too many people who neglect almost all other aspects of their lives because of work. They use work as an excuse for not doing many other important things. The belief suggested by their behavior is this: "Work is the most important thing in my life." Now, if you confront them with this belief, they may deny it. They say, "No, that's not at all true. There are lots of things that are more important than work." If you ask for some examples, they list things like family, religion, learning, friendships, and their health. But their actions don't support their argument. They frequently miss family activities (or don't schedule them at all) because of the demands "placed on them" by their jobs. Sometimes they even rationalize their actions by twisting this whole work-family relationship around, contending that "they only work hard so that they can provide for their family." Still, the fact remains, they don't spend time with their family. They also "don't have time" for worship, haven't read a good book in years, don't develop friendships outside their network of business acquaintances, and don't exercise. In other words, their behavior is a better indicator of what's on their belief window than their words are.

So, we've identified a very likely belief they have: "Work is the most important thing in my life." Once we've identified this belief, we can predict future behavior. How will a person operating on this assumption behave in the future? Just as he or she is now behaving. Will this meet his or her needs in the long term? No. Can we identify alternative beliefs that may yield better results? Of course we can. One of my favorites is a statement I heard so often in my youth that I'll never forget it: "No other success can compensate for failure in the home." Another might be: "On your death bed you're not going to wish you'd spent more time at the office." Or perhaps this one: "Knowledge is of value, even if it does not make me more effective at work." Can we predict future behavior based on these new beliefs? Of course we can. And we can also determine whether or not these new beliefs will likely meet an individual's basic needs better than the old one.

The real secret of this five-step formula, though, is not in applying it to someone else's life. The primary value of this process of improvement lies in applying it to ourselves. And that is not easy, for it requires us to be objective about our behavior and accept the beliefs our behavior shows are on our belief window, even if we'd rather not confront them. As I suggested when we talked about identifying governing values, your spouse or a trusted friend may provide valuable insights in helping you identify the beliefs written on your own belief window.

"I" Messages

That said, how do we go about helping someone else change a basic belief? Have you ever found yourself in the position of knowing that someone close to you—a family member or friend or work colleague— has an incorrect and destructive belief on his or her belief window, but doesn't know it? In other words, you can see the destructive behavior in action, you can predict the future results, but he or she is completely blind to all this. One of the most difficult challenges in life is to motivate another person to change. The reason for this is that *no one can make another person change*. We can persuade, plead, suggest, even demand, but if the other person does not want to alter his or her behavior, then no change will occur. The desire to change must come from within. How, then, can you help create that desire? Let me introduce you to a concept called the "I" message. The "I" message process has four distinct steps.

1. *Tell the other person, "I have a problem."*
2. *Give a nonthreatening description of the problem, from your viewpoint.*

3. *Tell the person how the situation makes **you** feel.*
4. *Let realities of the situation help produce the change.*

The first three steps are fairly straightforward and should create a climate in which the person is not feeling threatened. In step 4, two powerful questions need to be asked at this point: 1.) *If you continue this behavior, knowing how I feel about it, will it make our relationship better or worse?* and 2.) *Do you want our relationship to be better or worse?* These two questions can be used in any situation and, unless there is pathology present, will promote an honest and forthright response and exchange.

Let's assume, for the sake of an example, that your name is Kim. Let's also assume that you work for me, and you've been late for work every day for the last ten days. I'm your boss, I'm concerned, and I'm going to give you an "I" message. I would probably say something like this: "Kim, I have a problem. I've noticed (step 2) that you've been late for work for the past ten days. I need you to know (step 3) that I am very uncomfortable about the fact that you're late every day. Kim, if you continue this behavior, being late every day, knowing how I feel about it, will it make our relationship better or worse?" The magic question is this: If you continue this behavior, will it make our relationship better or worse? This causes you to put your behavior in the context of meeting your needs. And this leads to the final question.

"Kim, do you want our relationship to be better or worse?" Nine times out of ten the answer will be "better." Now, if you don't care about our relationship, if you want to have an argument, what will you say? "Worse." And what will happen? You'll lose your job. Will that meet your needs? Very rarely.

Usually you will say, "I want the relationship to be better." And I will say, "Well, if you want our relationship to improve, what are you going to have to do? You're going to have to change the belief on your belief window which says, 'Being late for work doesn't matter.' " The new belief that replaces the old one may look something like this: "Being late will cause tension between me and my boss, which in turn will not meet my needs in the long term."

I taught this concept of the "I" message to my children several years ago. I have a daughter, Stacie, a bright, wonderful young lady, who was in the ninth grade at the time. She played in the band that year, and this was very important to her. Now, my work causes me to be gone from home quite often. So, one day, Stacie came down to my office, which at that time was in the basement of my home, poked her head through the door and said, "Dad, I have a problem."

The minute she opened her mouth, I knew I'd been had, and I said, "Well, Stacie, maybe we'd better talk about it."

"Great." She walked into my office, sat across the desk from me, put her elbows on the desktop and repeated, "Dad, I have a problem." Step 1. Then she said, "I play in the school band. We have programs quite often over at the junior high. Because you travel all the time, you never come to the programs when I perform." Step 2, a nonthreatening description of my behavior. Was I aware of what her problem was? Yeah.

Then she went on to step 3. "I need you to understand, Dad, that when you're not at my programs, I really feel bad, and all the other kids kind of make fun because my dad's never there." Then came step 4. "Dad, if you continue this behavior of not being at my programs, will it make our relationship better or worse?"

I was on the floor at this point. I said very quietly, "Make it worse."

She said, "I just have one more question, Dad. Do you want our relationship to be better or worse?" And then she stood up and walked out.

Two days later she had a band concert at the junior high. Dad canceled three seminars. I was in the front row at that concert—because she had reminded me of a basic belief that I had somehow erased from my belief window, that my relationship with my kids is only as good as the degree of involvement I have in their lives. It went back on my window in a major way.

Now, it all started because in a nonthreatening way we were able to sit down together and, instead of attacking each other, were able to attack something else, the real cause of her frustration: my behavior. I hope you understand this. Your behavior is not *you*. If I say that your behavior is causing me pain, this is not saying that you are a bad person. I'm merely saying that you may be acting on an incorrect, perhaps hurtful belief. Because of this experience, Stacie and I have had some wonderful conversations about belief windows and how they drive behavior.

This is a very simple tool. You sit down and say, "Todd, I have a problem. My problem happens to be that we have a curfew at our home, and you're expected to be in by midnight, but you're never home at twelve. I feel uncomfortable about that. I worry myself sick about why you're gone. If you continue coming in after midnight, is it going to make our relationship better or worse?" This is how we start talking about behavior and how behavior can change.

The Reality Model is a powerful tool, not just for analyzing our own behavior and the results it brings us, but also for helping other people feel good about making needed changes in their behavior. It is an effective vehicle for improving our relationships with others.

The Reality Model separates what we do from what we are, for the two really are separate. If we can attack incorrect beliefs and destructive behavior without attacking ourselves or others, we can solve most of the human relations and personal productivity problems we encounter in life, and we can feel good about ourselves.

But, you say, aren't there some problems that are much deeper and vastly more difficult to come to grips with and solve? What about addiction and other seriously self-defeating behaviors? Will the Reality Model work in these cases? That's one of the issues we will look at in Law 8.

LAW 8

Negative behaviors
are overcome by changing
incorrect beliefs

As the Reality Model shows us, our behavior is strongly influenced by what we've put on our belief window. Regardless of whether or not our beliefs are correct (in line with reality), incorrect (not reflective of reality), or matters of opinion or preference, we assume that all of them are correct beliefs and we behave in accordance with them. Beliefs that really are correct will produce positive behavior, or behavior that achieves desired results. Conversely, incorrect beliefs will produce negative, self-defeating behavior that messes up our attempts to implement the ten natural laws discussed in this book. Left unchecked, negative behaviors will defeat your best attempts to take control of your life.

Negative behaviors can cover a wide spectrum, ranging from the mildly negative (yelling at your kids, telling "white" lies, overworking, etc.) to the strongly negative (substance abuse, spouse or child abuse, anorexia, compulsive lying, etc.). In extreme forms, negative behavior can be hurtful and destructive, both to the individual and to other people.

Too often, negative behavior seems unexplainable to us ("Why did I just do that?") or it is explained in behavioral science terms that we can't understand either. Here's where the Reality Model can provide some important "aha's" and insights that can help us avoid or overcome negative behavior.

Any negative behavior shows lack of control. It is a symptom of a reactive way of life. Negative behavior is often the result of trying to meet needs with incorrect or inappropriate beliefs on our belief window. Because the beliefs are not rooted in reality, they cannot produce behavior and results that will satisfy the unmet need. As we try ever harder to apply the inappropriate behavior in our attempt to satisfy the need, we can get trapped in a vicious downward spiral.

Take gossiping, for example. This common negative behavior springs mainly from the need to feel important and perhaps also from a twisted version of the need to be loved. Some people gossip to pull others down, assuming that stepping on someone else is the best way to move up in the world. Others gossip not to pull people down, but to drop names, leading their listeners to believe that they orbit in high social circles. Whatever the need that drives this behavior, however, and whatever short-term fulfillment it provides for that unmet need, the long-term damage is inevitable.

Gossip may make us feel important for a brief instant, may even bring us the momentary admiration of others, but admiration isn't love, and pulling others down will eventually catch up with us. In the long term we will have both a host of enemies, people we've stabbed in the back, and a reputation that may be impossible to get rid of. And this is typical of negative behavior. The unmet need that craves short-term fulfillment is the same need that winds up deprived in the long run.

In its extreme form, negative behavior is addictive behavior. When you see or hear the words "addictive behavior," what comes to mind? Unless you've been living on Pluto for the past thirty years, your first thought is probably drug or alcohol abuse. These are the news-making addictions of our day, and they are indeed serious behavior problems. Addictive behavior has been defined by one psychologist as *compulsive behavior with short-term benefits and long-term destruction*. Addiction to drugs and alcohol are just two of the more serious and visible of a whole range of negative behaviors we see in ourselves and others. This isn't a book about recovery from addiction, nor do I pretend to be an expert in combatting these major social and behavioral problems of our day. But the larger turf of which they are a part—negative behaviors—can often be more clearly seen and understood through the insights provided by the Reality Model.

Many negative behaviors not usually thought of as addictive differ from addictive behavior only in degree of compulsion and destructive results. In addition to drug and alcohol abuse, what other kinds of behaviors could be considered as addictive?

Overeating
Overworking
Smoking
Bragging
Sleeping
Shopping
Gossiping
Child and spouse abuse
Yelling at your kids
Telling crude jokes
Running

You're probably saying, "Come on, now! Some of those aren't what I think of as addictive behavior." Running, you ask? Yes, even exercise can be an addiction, if it becomes compulsive. When that happens, long-term negative effects can result. For example, if you insist on running five miles a day, even though this will aggravate an old knee injury, you may strengthen your cardiovascular system, but you may also permanently destroy your cartilage. Similarly, if every evening after dinner your spouse says, "Your turn to clean up the dishes," and you respond, "Sorry, I've gotta go work out—gotta keep in shape, you know," then you may eventually look like Arnold Schwarzenegger, but your marriage probably won't even be around in the long term. Short-term benefits, long-term destruction. Addiction, negative behaviors. It's surprising how many behaviors fit the definition to some degree.

Take yelling at your kids, for instance. What are the short-term benefits? Well, you get whatever's bothering you off your chest. Maybe you feel like you've done your small part in making the world a better place. Perhaps you suppress, at least for the moment, the objectionable behavior in your children. You may even enhance your sense of being in control.

But what are the long-term consequences? Your children will likely feel alienated. They may rebel. They may harbor long-festering grudges. They may even neglect you when you slip into the dependency of old age. Or they may mistakenly learn that anger is the appropriate response to other people's misconduct.

So, how can we overcome negative behavior in our own lives? How can we help others overcome their long-term destructive behaviors? Some of the answers to these questions lie in the Reality Model. The first step, of course, is coming to grips with the fact that we have a problem. The second step is recognizing that we have an unmet need which is driving that behavior. Then we can usually identify one or more incorrect beliefs, beliefs we have picked up somewhere that we think are satisfying that need, at least in the short term. And finally, we have to replace those beliefs with correct ones. Once we do that, if we are committed to the new beliefs, then changed behavior should happen automatically.

"Drugs and Alcohol Are Fun"

I was sitting in my office one day when a call came in from Brent Ward, the U.S. Attorney for the district of Utah. I had never met him before, but he said, "Hyrum, I'm tired of locking kids up for drug and alcohol abuse. I've decided to go to every high school in this state and put on an assembly. The Utah Jazz have agreed to send a basketball player with us. We've got a film we're going to show. Would you like to go with us and teach these kids how to get control of their lives?"

Well, I got excited about that. I said, "Brent, let's go for it."

In a three-year period we put on assemblies in high schools all over Utah. On one particular day, though, Brent Ward was not able to go. He was in Washington. So he sent one of his assistant U.S. attorneys. The Utah Jazz basketball team was also on the road. So the assistant U.S. attorney and I went alone. We went to the high school, walked through the front door, the principal met us, took us into his office, sat us down, and said, "Now, you guys are used to talking to the whole student body, right?" Then he said, "Well, I don't want you to talk to the whole student body. They're not the ones who have the problem. I want you to talk to our druggies and alcoholics."

I said, "You know who they are?"

"Yeah, I know who they are."

He took us to a band room and left us there. There was only one door, and the chairs rose up away from the front of the room where we sat. After a few minutes the bell rang, the door opened, and in walked fifty of the hardest-looking kids I've ever seen. One kid had a ring through his nose. Another had green hair that stood straight up.

The principal came through the door and walked to the front of the room. And before he could open his mouth, a kid jumped out of his chair, obviously a ring leader, and said, "Hey, how come we're all in here, anyway?" The principal said, "Because you're all druggies and alcoholics, and these two guys are going to fix it."

Now, I've had lots of introductions in my life, but that was the most interesting one. The principal turned around and walked out. He didn't even want to watch.

When I got to the front of the room, I noticed this long-haired kid draped across three chairs. He had on these funky glasses with spirals in them. This kid was feeling no pain whatsoever. And for some reason I decided to take him on. I said, "Well, it looks like we have our class nerd here."

He jumped out of his chair, tore his glasses off, and said, "I don't have to take that."

I said, "That's right, you don't. Why don't you get out?"

He said, "Okay, I will." He stormed over to the door, turned around, swore at me—three words I'd really never heard before—and slammed the door.

When he slammed the door, the rest of the class said, again almost in one voice, "Hey, get the guy with the suit!"

I had to shout at them, because they were making so much noise. I yelled, "Now give me your attention. I came here to teach you about something called the Reality Model. You're going to commit it to memory before you walk out that door. You're going to have it burned in your brains. You got that?"

Venomous stares.

"I don't have a blackboard up here," I said, "so I'm going to need five volunteers." With a little cajoling, I eventually got five kids sitting up front, each representing a piece of the model. J.D., the kid who had accosted the principal, sat in one of the chairs, representing the belief window on the model. "All right," I said, "I'm going to give you a belief you might have on your belief window. Here it is: '*My self-worth is dependent on being okay with my friends.*' " Do you know any young people who have that belief on their belief window? Any older people?

When I asked for someone to suggest what need might be driving that belief, a kid pops up, "To feel important," in a smart-alecky tone. I said, "Yeah, and how about to be loved. Maybe there are two needs driving that belief. And if that's true, then your self-worth is not okay unless your friends say you're okay. What if you go to a party and your friends offer you drugs and alcohol? What are you going to do?"

Almost in unison, they said, "Hey man, we're going to do it."

I said, "Right, you're going to do it. Are the results of that going to meet your needs over time?" Blank stares. They didn't even know what I was talking about.

But we started driving stuff through the model. We were twenty-five minutes into this when J.D., my belief window, jumped out of his chair. Suddenly the class went dead quiet. I could see everybody thinking, "Man, J.D.'s going to get the guy with the suit!"

But instead he said, "Let me tell you how stupid this model is. You just told us if the results of our behavior don't meet our needs, there's an incorrect belief on our belief window. That means that if the results of our behavior *do* meet our needs, we have a *correct* belief on our window. Right?"

I was excited, because he used the words of the model perfectly. "Right!" I said, and I knew exactly where he was going, so I stopped him and said, "Now, wait a minute, J.D. Do you drink?"

"Yeah, I drink."

"How much do you drink?"

"Eight or ten beers a week. Get smashed on weekends."

"You get smashed every weekend?"

"Yeah."

"Are you an alcoholic?"

"No way, man. You can't be an alcoholic drinking like that."

I said, "You just gave me one of the things written on your belief window."

"I did?"

"Yeah, you did. You just told me you believe you can take eight beers a week and get smashed on weekends and you won't be an alcoholic. You just told me you believe that."

"So?"

"That's all. I just wanted to make sure you understand that. Go ahead, J.D."

"Okay, *Hy-rum*, I have a belief on my window. I don't care what my friends think about me. The belief on my window is 'Drugs and alcohol are fun.' And the need driving it? Variety, baby. Take that through your stupid model. If that's true, then I can set up my rules. I go to a party. My friends offer me drugs and alcohol. I take it. Do the results of that meet my needs? You bet they do. When I take drugs and alcohol, I feel terrific. That means I have a correct belief on my belief window, right?"

You could have heard a pin drop in that room. I stood there for about thirty seconds, then I said, "Right."

"Right?"

"Yeah, right. But you forgot something. Results take time to measure. You don't know yet. You may feel good that night, but over time is that going to meet your needs?"

And just like that he said, "Okay, okay. That means I take drugs and alcohol all my life and prove it, right?"

Bright kid. I said, "Yeah, you can do that if you want. But that's the dumbest way to find out if you've got a correct belief on your window."

He said, "How else are you going to do it?"

"You can take a look at somebody else's life who took drugs and alcohol his whole life and see if it really met his needs. Can we do that?"

"Yeah."

"Okay, J.D." Now, at this point we were nose to nose and I was sweating bullets. I said, "You give me one example of somebody who took drugs and alcohol his whole life and it really met his needs. You give me one example."

The example he gave me was Elvis Presley. I said, "Presley? Where's Presley, for crying out loud?"

"Dead."

"How come?"

"OD'd on drugs."

"That meet his needs?"

J.D. sat down.

Now, for the first time I had their undivided attention. I said, "Now, listen carefully. I didn't come down here to tell you *what* belongs on your belief window. That's none of my business. I came here to tell you that you *have* a belief window, you have the same four needs that I have, and you're putting beliefs that you *think* are going to meet your needs on that belief window every day. Are you mature enough to take that window off, see if those beliefs are correct, and change the ones that aren't working?" A few heads started to nod.

They were starting to think, "Maybe there's something to this." Earlier, I had made this one important point: When you observe a pattern of behavior, you can tell what's on the person's belief window. And more scary than that, if you know what's on someone's belief window, you can predict behavior with great accuracy. And if you can predict behavior, what else can you predict? Results. Now I figured I could get away with something. I said, "Listen up, guys. Remember, I told you that if you observe a pattern of behavior, you can tell what's on that person's belief window, right?"

All heads nodded. "Yeah, man, that's right."

I said, "Okay, I'm standing here observing a pattern of behavior." Then I pointed at a long-haired kid and said, "You, get up." He stood up, defiant as can be, hair down below his shoulders. "You're wearing long hair."

"So?"

"How long have you been wearing long hair?"

"Five years."

"That makes it a pattern of behavior, right?"

"Yeah."

"There must be something on your belief window that's making you wear long hair. I want to know what it is."

This kid stood there for a full minute. At the end of the minute, this kid said quietly, and I'll never forget this, "Gets my father's attention."

Which of the four needs was not being met in this young man's life? Understand this very important fact: When any of those four needs is not being met, our energy flows toward meeting that need. And if we put an incorrect assumption on our belief window, it can cause behavior that may work in the short term. But in the long term it will destroy. Will we still behave that way, even if we understand the long-term consequences? Unfortunately, we will—unless we decide to break that cycle. It is very difficult for most people to look beyond the short term.

"Nobody Loves Her"

At this point J.D. jumped up. All the hostility was gone from him, and he said, "Okay, Hyrum, now here's the real thing." When he started talking about the "real thing," he started pacing back and forth in front of the class. "I have a friend. She's a girl. She's not my girlfriend." The class went deathly quiet. They all knew who he was talking about. "She's a cocaine addict, she's an alcoholic. Her parents are all screwed up. They're alcoholics. They beat her all the time. This girl is out there somewhere right now thinking about committing suicide. Hyrum, if that girl kills herself, we've wasted a life. We can't let her kill herself. How are we going to save this girl?"

Everybody in the room was expecting a golden answer from the guy in the suit. I just stood there and said, "I don't know."

"What do you mean, you don't know?"

"How am I supposed to know?" I said. "Let's plug what we know into the model. What's her behavior?"

"She's a cocaine addict; she's an alcoholic. I told you that already."

"Will the results of that behavior meet her needs over time?"

I then had the most electric teaching experience I have ever had. Sixty heads in the room shook back and forth. "You got that right," I said. "So what does that mean?"

"She's got a screwed-up belief window," suggested one kid.

Then J.D. said, "If I go home and tell her she's got a screwed-up belief window, she'll throw me out."

"Yeah," I said, "I think you're right. I don't think you can do that. But we know what's wrong, right? That means there's a need not being met. Let's go back a step. Which of the four needs isn't being met?"

A kid stood up over on the side. He had long hair and a scruffy beard, he was wearing an old army jacket. He looked like he was thirty-five. He was sixteen years old. He had his hands in his pockets. And he looked like he'd had a revelation. "Nobody loves her."

"That's interesting," I said. "So what do we do?"

Same kid, still on his feet, looking at me like I'm a complete idiot. "We love her, dummy."

"That's a great idea. How are we going to do that?"

These kids then came up with the most wonderful ways they could show this girl they loved her, things that would help build her self-esteem and hopefully bring her back from the brink.

"Do you think," I said, "if that need started being met some other way, maybe we could start talking to her about what's on her belief window?"

"Yeah."

At this point the bell rang again. Time's up. The principal came back in. He missed the whole thing, didn't even know what happened. J.D. got out of his chair, walked over to me, looked me in the eye, said, "Hyrum, I'll tell you something. I've been in and out of drug and alcohol therapy for ten years." This kid is sixteen. His brother had given him cocaine when he was six. He said, "I've been in jail four times. I've had every shrink in this state try and shrink me down. And this is the first time anything made any sense to me."

I looked at him and said, "J.D., I'm going to tell you one more time, I didn't come down here to tell you what belongs on your belief window. That's none of my business. I came down here to tell you you've got a belief window. You've got the same four needs I've got. And you're putting beliefs on that window every day, because you think they're going to meet your needs. Are you mature enough to take that window off, put it on the table, and find out if those beliefs are correct?"

He stood there, squared his shoulders, and said, "Yeah, I am."

And I looked at him and said, "Well, J.D., I guess we'll see, won't we?"

I've kept track of J.D. since that day, and so far he has been mature enough to replace some of his incorrect beliefs with correct ones. He graduated from high school and went on to college. He's doing something with his life, and I can guarantee you that his needs are being satisfied more fully than they were when he was a victim of his own addictive behavior.

There are two wonderful things about the Reality Model. One is that you can be very confrontive about attacking someone's belief window without attacking them. The other is that it places the responsibility for behavior on each individual. Personally, I don't buy into the argument some people use that says, "I'm screwed up because my parents screwed me up." We all reach the point in our lives, unless we are mentally or emotionally handicapped, where we are responsible for ourselves. We're responsible for what we've written on our belief window, and we have control over what we let stay on that window. Negative behavior is not something you have no control over. Very often it vanishes almost automatically when the incorrect belief that drives it is replaced by a correct belief.

As we have seen, the things written on our belief windows have a powerful influence not only on what we do, but how we feel about ourselves. More on this in the next natural law, Law 9.

LAW 9

Your self-esteem must ultimately come from within

"The eyes of other people," said Ben Franklin, "are the eyes that ruin us. If all but myself were blind, I should want neither fine clothes, fine houses, nor fine furniture." It is difficult to ignore the opinions of others, especially when we respect or admire them.

We all naturally seek to validate our feelings of self-worth. We want to feel good about ourselves, and we want others to think highly of us. Too often, though, this seeking of others' approval pressures us into behaving contrary to our deepest values. Thus, when we seek validations externally, we lose control over our lives. We behave according to someone else's values and principles rather than our own. And sometimes we are just guessing at what will please others. Then we find ourselves acting on nothing better than our own perception (or misperception) of their values. This is a highly reactive way of living, and is incredibly stressful.

"You're Ugly"

My good friend Bob Bennett, in teaching the concept of the belief window, once asked an audience to suppose that somewhere, sometime, someone they trusted told them they were ugly. (Haven't we all been told this, at least indirectly, at some point in our lives?) Bob used this example before a group including a particularly attractive girl—one you would notice as soon as she walked into a room. The only problem with this girl's appearance was that she never seemed to smile. When Bob mentioned this particular principle, she *really* didn't smile. And she didn't participate in any of the discussion that followed.

Afterward, her boyfriend approached Bob and wanted to talk. He said, incredibly, this girl *was* convinced that she was *ugly*. Her mother had told her this quite often when she was a child.

"I can't get her to accept the idea that she is attractive," the boyfriend said. "It's a major part of her self-esteem problem, and it's affecting our relationship."

Of course it affected their relationship. When he told her he thought she was attractive, she inwardly told herself, "He's either lying or he's too stupid to realize how ugly I really am." Neither trait, of course, was one that she wanted to have in a boyfriend.

By internalizing her mother's opinion and putting it on her own belief window, this young woman had given her mother control over this aspect of her life; she could not take control herself until she replaced her mother's viewpoint with one of her own.

If this young woman could accept the possibility that her mother might be wrong, she would probably discover that she is in fact beautiful—not only to her boyfriend, but to others as well—and that he is not lying when he insists that she is attractive. She could then take control of her feelings toward him, instead of allowing her mother to dominate their relationship from the grave.

Group Beliefs

Very often we let the social climate in which we live determine what we put on our own belief window. We accept the values of the larger group—whether it be a corporation or a neighborhood—without considering their impact on either our behavior or our feelings of self-worth. Let me illustrate.

In early 1989, Dr. Norman K. Spencer, principal of the Benjamin Franklin High School in Philadelphia, invited Franklin Quest to join in a partnership with his school. This school is an all-black high school in the middle of one of the most dangerous ghettos in the United States. As a result of this new partnership, and after having seen what Dr. Spencer had done with this school (which is a story all by itself), I was invited to speak to the junior and senior students on May 16, 1989.

The night before I was to speak, I was teaching a seminar for a major client in New Jersey. Whenever I go to Princeton, they pick me up in a limousine at the Newark Airport, drive me to Princeton and then back to the airport. But since I had to be in Philadelphia the next day, the limousine took me late that night to Philadelphia.

We drove through the section of town where the high school is located on our way to the hotel. It was, in fact, a very depressing part of the city. The poverty we saw as we drove in the stretch limousine was something to behold. The contrast of the limousine and the neighborhood we were driving through was a poignant experience for me.

The next morning I was escorted out to the high school. I was not allowed to travel to the school on my own because of the danger of the ghetto. I arrived at the high school and was greeted by Dr. Spencer, a wonderful human being. He explained to me as we entered the school that the doors were chained each morning at 8:30 A.M. to keep the drug pushers out of the school.

Prior to speaking to the student body, I had the opportunity of meeting with their president and the other student officers. I was wonderfully impressed with the caliber of these young black students. In the middle of all of this squalor and depression and ugliness, here were some students who somehow had been given hope by the experience they were having at this school. I attribute that success to Dr. Spencer and his staff.

I spent two hours in the auditorium that morning with nine hundred black students. I was probably the only white person within twenty-five blocks. I shared the Reality Model with them and we talked about belief windows. About ninety minutes into my presentation, I walked out into the auditorium with my microphone and approached one of the students sitting on the aisle. I said to him, "Suppose you lived in a neighborhood where the neighborhood belief window contained the assumption, "All blacks are stupid." At that point you could hear a pin drop in the auditorium. The air got so thick you could taste it. Nine hundred students were on the edge of their seats.

This young man looked at me, squared his shoulders, lifted his head up and said, "All blacks *aren't* stupid."

I then said, "I didn't say they were. I said, suppose you lived in a neighborhood where that was the prevailing view."

In the same position and posture as before, this young man repeated, "All blacks *aren't* stupid."

It took me four times before he understood what we were doing. When he finally understood that I was not attacking him, he said to me (and I will never forget this as long as I live), "I live in a neighborhood like that!"

I asked him, "How much fun is that?"

He said, "It's no fun."

I turned to the students in the room and made this point. I said, "Our prejudgments—and that's exactly what prejudice is—are deep-seated opinions we have placed on our belief windows. Because we believe them to be true, those prejudices drive behavior that inflicts tremendous pain on people throughout the world. Whenever we say 'all blacks are . . . ,' 'all Hispanics are . . . ,' 'all women are . . . ,' 'all professional athletes are . . . ,' we're increasing the level of pain in the world." And whenever we accept someone else's prejudice against us, that we are inferior in any way, we give them a degree of control in our lives and our sense of self-worth suffers.

I grew up in the Hawaiian Islands where I was, in fact, in the minority. In my graduating class in high school, there were only five Caucasians— *Haoles*, as we were referred to—out of a graduating class of sixty. The rest of that class were Polynesians and Orientals, mostly Orientals.

It never occurred to me as I was growing up in that wonderful atmosphere that I had any call to be prejudiced, or that I was in any way inferior to those in the racial majority. I was the minority, but I had to come to the mainland to discover what prejudice was really all about.

Wouldn't it be wonderful if young people, as they grow up in this great country, could remove prejudices from their belief windows? But even if that doesn't happen, we don't have to accept judgments that demean us or make us feel inferior. What other people believe doesn't affect how I feel about myself unless I accept their beliefs. I can be happy and successful, regardless of other people's opinions.

You Are a Ten

If you truly want to gain control of your life, there's one concept that you must put on your belief window. It has to do with you as an individual and you in whatever roles you may find yourself. The diagram below represents you, the human being, as the center circle and the various roles you play in the outer circles.

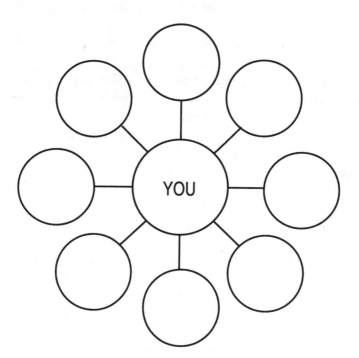

If you want, you can write your name in the center circle. In the outer, "satellite" circles, however, I'd like you to write the various roles you find yourself in—father, mother, spouse, manager, employee, friend, brother, sister, son, daughter, coach, team member, student, teacher, etc. Now, if you wanted to spend enough time, you could identify literally hundreds of different roles that you play. You go into the kitchen to cook something, you become a cook. You walk through the door of a store, you become a customer. You go to a city council meeting to voice your opinion on some issue, you become a concerned citizen. You donate money to a good cause, you become a patron or benefactor. You spend time working at the local homeless shelter, you become a volunteer. There are hundreds of roles you play.

Now, if I were to ask you to rate your performance in each of those roles from one to ten—one being terrible, ten being fantastic—how would you rate yourself? In other words, you ask yourself, "On a scale from one to ten, what kind of friend am I? What kind of brother am I? What kind of daughter am I? What kind of employee am I? If you're like most people, you'd give yourself a score somewhere between four and eight for nearly every role. Why is this? Because practically none of us think of ourselves as terrible. Maybe we're not great, but we're not that bad. As employees, for instance, even if we arrive late for work, leave early, and fool around a little while we're there, we're still not all that bad—at least a four. Just a bit below average. Maybe we're not the best parents in the world, but we try hard. Our kids might think we're a one or two, but we see the whole picture—we look at our intentions, balance our strengths and weaknesses, and logically conclude that we're at least a four. And in some things, we're pretty good, impressive even. A ten? No, probably not. Maybe not even a nine. But definitely a seven or eight. We're great neighbors, for instance. Just ask anybody. We're modest too. That's why we hardly ever give ourselves a nine or ten. We're not perfect, but we sometimes come marvelously close.

This role rating is an interesting exercise, especially when spouses compare answers. It creates some wonderful conversation.

Now, I want you to do the same thing with the center circle. If you were to give yourself a rating, from one to ten, what would it be? If you consider yourself as a human being, apart from any particular role, what are you? Do you know what most people put in that center circle? Well, it's never a ten. And generally it's lower than some of the scores in the outer circles, the role scores. Many people don't feel so great about themselves as human beings. "I'm a pretty good employee," they might say to themselves, "but there's nothing special about me as an individual."

I want you to pay particular attention to the next statement, because it may be the most important idea in the whole book. *If you did not place a ten in the center circle, you do not have the capacity to be a ten in any of the outer circles.* The point here is this: I do not believe the good Lord made any "seven," "eight," or "nine" human beings. All he made was tens. We're not tens in the roles we play yet. That's our task in life. But if I believe—and this is a belief window issue—that I'm a "seven" human being, will I ever be a "nine" employee? No. It is physically, emotionally, mentally impossible. I can't do it. But the fact is, we are all tens. We may not act like it very often, but in terms of our potential, we definitely are tens. And once we accept that, once we write that belief indelibly on our belief windows, we will have an infinitely greater chance of acting like tens, of becoming "ten" fathers, mothers, spouses, friends, employees, and neighbors.

There is always a gap between the ideal and the real. Our performance is never perfect. That's fine. The important thing is that we are narrowing the distance between where we are and where we should be. There are two ways we can narrow that distance, though. We can either lower the standard, the ideal—in other words, declare that we can never become tens—or we can raise our performance. Lowering the ideal is a cop-out. Yes, we may feel a bit better about ourselves, some of our frustration may fade away, but we will also feel rather empty. We always feel empty when we forsake our dreams, our true values and goals. And that is exactly what lowering the ideal does—it dilutes our values and goals. It tells us we can never be a ten because we've accepted the lie that becoming a ten is impossible.

The only path to inner peace is to set those values and goals—the ideals we cherish—permanently in our minds, refuse to compromise them, and work diligently to bring our performance nearer to that level. It isn't easy, but it is possible. We have the potential to become tens in the roles we play. And we have that potential because we *are* tens as human beings. If, in doing this exercise yourself, you placed a number less than ten in the center circle, you have until the end of the chapter to change it to a ten.

Conforming to YOU

As we've discussed self-esteem to this point, I hope you have come to understand two fundamental principles about yourself. First, *what's written on your belief window about yourself has a powerful effect on your self-esteem*, both positively and negatively. Second, *as human beings, we are all tens.* These two principles often fight each other inside us. Feelings deep within us confirm the presence of something transcendent at the center of our souls; but at the same time something else keeps trying to convince us that we're really worthless, that we don't matter. Listening to our intuitions of something divine within us leads us toward the inner peace we all seek.

Giving in to the feelings of worthlessness can lead to depression and despair, crippling the natural abilities and unique potentials we each possess.

I also firmly believe that our individual success and fulfillment depends to a significant degree on our outlook; we each make our own luck. But it's not a luck that happens by chance. It happens when we let the natural power within us flow out and provide power that leads to success. Recent studies of athletes tell of times when they experience a "flow" of super performance beyond their natural ability. They describe feelings like being in slow motion, with a vivid clarity of what they are doing, and knowing that they will get the goal or otherwise succeed in their effort. These athletes having "flow" experiences or playing "in the zone" can't force such performance; it usually must flow naturally out of them. To some degree, this process can take place in each of us, if we learn how to let it happen. Let me illustrate.

Have you ever noticed that many people seem to consistently have things turn out badly, while others seem to live a charmed life—everything goes well for them. It doesn't matter how conscientious or sincere the people are—one group's bread always seems to fall jelly side down, while for the other group it falls jelly side up.

A good friend of mine tells of two acquaintances who illustrate this contrast. One man has always wanted the same thing—money. He has tried many ways to achieve this desire over the years and none has ever really worked. He is sincere, diligent, smart, hard-working. But things never quite seem to work for him; he is just getting by financially. Making matters worse is a colleague at work who is *always* making money—without even trying. In one venture he bought some property for very little and sold it for a huge profit. And to top it off, after he had used the money to pay off his mortgage and buy several new cars, the property reverted back to him because the developer couldn't make the payments. At this same time, the first man bought property and ended up losing his shirt. The first man says the colleague is "crazy like a fox," but people who have known him for years say that none of it is planned. Much of the time he hardly seems to be on this planet; he just moseys through life almost oblivious—and having everything work for him.

This isn't so unusual. Most of us know of people like my friend's two acquaintances. The important question is: What makes the difference? Why do some people seem to have a certain magic, an uncanny ability to be at the right place at the right time, and are always falling into opportunities and successes seemingly by accident—while the rest of us watch in disbelief and frustration?

I'd like to suggest an answer: Conformity. Now, you're probably saying, "You've got to be kidding! This is a joke, right?" But let me explain with a little example. At a gathering of conservative, eight-to-five accountants with buttondown shirts, two cars, and a spouse and family, those with similar dress and demographics would be *conforming* to the group norms and expectations. An accountant attending the gathering who dressed like a hippie and lived in a commune would be a *nonconformist*.

Now, let's turn the example on end. If that same hippie accountant were to attend a gathering of "Alternative Life-style Accountants," he or she would be one who was conforming. One of the buttondown group attending the meeting would be the nonconformist. Conformity, you see, is totally relative to the context or situation.

The kind of conformity that doesn't work is when we try to follow what others are doing when it goes against our own instincts and values. Conformity of this kind too often puts blinders on us. We're so busy following the others that don't see opportunities and solutions to problems that are right there if we would just look around. In many ways, it's like standing in front of a brick wall and pounding your head against it, thinking that if you just try harder and pound longer, you'll somehow break through.

If you frequently find yourself pounding at the wall, you may have the following belief on your belief window: "To find fulfillment (being happy, rich, successful, or whatever) I must conform to what these other people say I need to be or do." It doesn't matter who the other people are—friends, classmates at school, work colleagues, peer group, acquaintances at church—if we look to them for validation of our self-worth and accept their values as absolutely true, we give control of our lives to them, without even questioning or realizing that we have lost it.

Blind acceptance at its worst has given us the Spanish Inquisition and the Holocaust; at the very least it has given us shallow and wasted lives. Henry David Thoreau once said: "The mass of men lead lives of quiet desperation." That desperation comes from conforming to other people's values and ideals. Thoreau also said: "If a man does not keep pace with his companions, perhaps it is because he hears a different drummer. Let him step to the music which he hears, however measured or far away."

This is excellent counsel. In fact, it is the secret to that magic we talked about earlier.

And this brings us back to the wall. Pounding your head against it is nothing more than trying to get someone else's values to work for you. It *should* work, we reason, but it doesn't. At least not nearly so easily as using a more realistic method of getting through the wall. You see, there's a door not far from where you're banging your head. And you don't need a key to open it. There isn't even a lock. But to go through that door you must accept a different assumption: "To find fulfillment, I must conform to my own uniqueness, and march to the drummer of my own values. My happiness and success depend on my being myself and living up to my unique potential." I call this idea "Conforming to YOU" (Your Own Uniqueness).

This sounds simple, but walking down the wall to the door isn't easy. It may require major changes in thinking. You can no longer have the comfort of saying that your failures are really someone else's fault. You realize that you alone are responsible for your own success and failure.

More than we care to admit, we like to control each other, to project on others what we think they should do, think, or be. And even more disturbing is the fact that we ourselves often love to be controlled. We crave the security that conforming to others' values gives us. But as with all incorrect beliefs, we don't like some of the results that spring from that behavior.

The underlying theme of this entire book is gaining control of *your* life—not anyone else's, yours. You are unique, and if you lose control of your life, you also lose your uniqueness, you become a dim reflection of someone else's personality. True success in life can only come when you are true to the uniqueness in you.

Your car has more than fifteen thousand parts in it. Obviously, each of those parts is unique. You can't make a car from fifteen thousand dip-sticks or fifteen thousand steering wheels. But with fifteen thousand unique parts functioning together, you get magic—a machine that will move at sixty-five miles per hour for over one hundred thousand miles. The same magic exists in all mechanical and living systems. We wouldn't try to turn fifteen thousand different auto parts into identical ones, so why do we deny the magic by trying to make other people into clones of ourselves, or worse, make ourselves into clones of someone else? For any organization—be it as large as the American society or as small as a family—to work correctly, we must recognize and enhance the uniqueness of each individual member.

I'd like you to take a moment and think of three individuals that you admire. They may be historical or noted people such as Lincoln or Churchill or Mother Theresa, or simply people you know who have traits you would like to emulate. Now ask yourself this: Did any of these people conform to other people's values? My guess is that part of why you admire them lies in the fact that they were (or are) true to themselves—they conform to their own uniqueness.

The "other people" don't always like those who walk to the beat of a different drummer. They try to control them, and sometimes even kill them. You may pay a heavy price to walk along the wall and through the doorway. But there is a magic that comes when you do it. R. Buckminster Fuller, the inventive genius that created the easily constructed geodesic dome, once said that when he followed his own vision, things worked. But when he did what most people did and got a regular job, things went sour. In my own life, I have found that when I follow my own dreams, the magic is there. The coincidences of people, resources, and opportunities seem to magically fall into place. When I follow the crowd, the magic vanishes.

There are two questions you can ask yourself to help you find the magic:

1. What do I *really* want? This is a hard question to answer. It revolves around your core values. Expect some pain as you sift through the "should-haves" and "ought-tos" until you reach the things that really matter to you.
2. What has worked for me in the past? Remember those times in the past when you did have the magic and things worked. Identify any common patterns: the kinds of situations, the people who were involved, the specifics of what you did. Your future successes may result from repeating those patterns.

Three Levels of Motivation

To help you understand the emotions that are behind many of our motivations, let me introduce you to an idea developed by Kay Allan in his book, *The Journey From Fear to Love*. If we look beyond the emotions of passion—greed, anger, revenge, lust, etc.—Allan notes that there are three major emotions that motivate us in most of our actions: fear, duty, and love. These emotions may be ranked in terms of how personally satisfying and fulfilling they are; there's a less fulfilling emotion, a middle-of-the-road emotion, and a higher or more fulfilling emotion. No matter what you're doing, unless you're completely on autopilot, or acting out of passion or habit, you are usually functioning under one of these emotions.

The lowest level of motivation, of course, is **fear**. The feeling that surfaces at the fear level is: I *have* to do this. Some people come to work in the morning out of fear, and perform many of their daily tasks out of fear. There's a penalty waiting out there if they don't perform. Some of us even take our spouses out to dinner out of fear.

Fear is a subtle emotion. Some people are overprotective of their children, not necessarily because they love them, but because they are afraid of what might happen to them in the great, wide world. Some people get into careers that cause them immense frustration because they are afraid of what their father or mother might think if they follow their dreams.

Fear is a great motivator. The only problem with it is that it makes the person who's experiencing it feel terrible. Why does it make us feel terrible? Because it is an external source of motivation. We are reacting to someone else's values when we act out of fear. Fear is perhaps the ultimate reactive mode. And when we are reactive, we have given up control of our lives. When I do something out of fear, who is controlling my life? Whoever is holding the penalty over my head.

The second level of motivation stems from **duty**, our sense of responsibility. The feeling that surfaces here is: I *ought* to do this. Many people function day in, day out, on their sense of duty. They do things because they feel it is their obligation, not because they want to do them. They generally have commendable values, especially a highly developed sense of fairness. "I put in a full day's work for a full day's pay, because it's the honorable thing to do." "I work hard to support my family, because they deserve the best I can provide." "I donate money to the Boy Scouts because that organization helped me stay out of trouble as a youth."

Duty is a more fulfilling motivator than fear, but it is still an external motivation. Who makes us feel a responsibility to do something? Well, part of its springs from our sense of honor, but our sense of honor would be perfectly content to lie dormant if someone weren't holding the other end of the rope we call obligation. We can feel them there. Now and then there's an almost imperceptible tug on the rope. We owe them something. And our sense of duty makes us uncomfortable unless we pay up. I owe my boss a fair day's work, because he pays me. In a very real way, he's controlling my behavior—through my sense of duty. I may not love my work, but I ought to do my best—it's my duty. So I plod along, giving my time and energy and intelligence but not my heart.

This is still a far cry from the highest and most fulfilling level of motivation, **love**. You see, love inspires a different kind of behavior than either duty or fear. If I love my work, I don't do it for anyone else. I do it because I love it; I *want* to do it. I revel in it and, chances are, I will have much success and satisfaction in it. If I love my children instead of fearing for them, I don't restrict them with unrealistic requirements. I trust them. I teach them. And I let them go out into the great, wide world, prepared and eager to live their own lives.

Stress

I mentioned earlier that living according to someone else's values is a highly reactive way of life, and the reactive mode is extremely stressful. Whenever we follow a principle that isn't right for us, that we have picked up from someone else, we create an inner conflict that produces stress. Let me illustrate with an example from my own life.

Several years ago I met a wonderful human being who was doing seminars and consulting work at the Merrill Lynch Corporation. This man was Dr. Robert Eliot, a cardiovascular surgeon who himself had had a heart attack. Consequently, he was very familiar with what one goes through when one has had that experience, and he has pioneered much of the research on the connection between stress and heart disease.

Dr. Eliot did a number of studies discovering what causes stress in people's lives and later created an institute where executives could go to be tested to determine whether they are *hot* or *cold* reactors and to help them achieve the correct balance and avoid heart disease. Before I tell you about my own experience, I'd like you to understand the difference between a hot and a cold reactor. When people experience stress, which everyone experiences to one degree or another, the cardiovascular system reacts in a certain way. For example, when you experience stress, the veins in your body which carry blood stretch out much like a garden hose. If you took a hose and tied it between two vehicles and pulled it tight, the cars would stretch out the hose and the opening would become smaller. That is exactly what happens to the veins in our bodies when we experience stress. This happens to everyone. However, the difference between a hot and cold reactor is what our heart does in the stressful situation.

When the veins constrict under stress in a hot reactor, the heart will increase its rate and try to force more blood through the now smaller diameter of the artery. This causes the blood pressure to go up and, hence, the label of hot reactor. On the other hand, when the stress occurs in a cool reactor, instead of the heart pumping harder and faster trying to force more blood through a smaller hole, the heart will slow down and force less blood through that smaller constricted area. Thus, the label known as cool reactor. People who are cool reactors obviously have much less likelihood of strokes and heart attacks because they are not overburdening their cardiovascular systems in a stressful situation.

The wonderful thing about this whole process is that we can, in fact, train our bodies to function as cool reactors. When we are under stress, we can reduce the amount of blood that we are forcing through the veins consciously. Just the fact that this is even possible is very exciting to me.

After understanding the hot and cool reactor concept, I decided that I would visit Dr. Eliot's Institute of Fitness to determine what type of reactor I was. The testing takes one and a half days to complete. You check in the night before the testing actually starts. The next morning you are advised what you will be eating for the next day and a half. Then for eight solid hours they go through your body almost as if you had checked it into a garage.

They gave me all kinds of tests. They put me on a treadmill, hooked me up to fifteen different electrodes, raised the treadmill, stepped it up so my heart was beating like crazy, then put me into a room. This was a very interesting experience for me. I sat in a chair and experienced simulated stressful events to determine what my cardiovascular system did under stress. Again, I was hooked up to at least fourteen different electronic monitors attached to my body. I was alone in the room with a television screen. A talking head came onto the screen and proceeded to say that there were three tests they were going to put me through that would simulate stressful situations. They would be monitoring my cardio-vascular system in the next room and I was to follow the instructions as carefully as possible.

Please understand that I had already gone through the treadmill test, so they had discovered what my cardiovascular system did under physical stress. The stress I was now going to be exposed to was mental and emotional stress. The first test they had me do was play a pong game on the video screen. It was a classic game where a little ball drops from the top of the screen and I was to catch it with a little tray at the bottom using the toggle switch on the chair I was seated in. They explained this game would last for about sixty to ninety seconds and I should do my best to catch that ball every time it came down. The game started, and it was much like the video games that children play today. As this little ball kept dropping off the screen and I would catch it, it seemed to increase in speed. It kept getting faster and faster and faster. I had to move the toggle switch faster and faster, and I was having a great time. All the while in the next room, the needles were tracing patterns on a graph, describing electronically what my cardiovascular system was doing.

The next test the talking head on the monitor asked me to do was to count backward from 777 subtracting by 7 verbally, aloud, as fast as I could. I was asked to be accurate and continue for one minute counting back as far as I could go. They asked if I was ready, and when I replied that I was, I was told to start. So, I started to subtract. I went 777, 770, 763, etc. I did not do this exceptionally fast. I discovered that accuracy was more important to me and I counted backward somewhat slowly as far as I could. I don't remember how far I counted backward but I went back to a pretty good number. At the end of the minute, the talking head came back onto the screen and stated this test was completed.

The head informed me that the final test they would conduct would use the bucket of ice that was sitting next to my chair. Up to that point, I had not noticed the bucket of ice, but on my right there it was, a regular #10 bucket, full of ice water with a towel draped over it. The head asked me to take the towel off the bucket and to notice it was full of ice and water. The head explained that this test would require me to put my whole right arm into this bucket and leave it there for sixty seconds. This can be very painful, and I was advised if I needed to take my hand out of the ice water before the sixty seconds were up that I was to do so, but to please warn them before doing so.

Then, before this test started, the head said, "Now understand that this may be a little painful. Most people are able to do this, so don't worry about it." That became an immediate challenge to me. I was thinking if everyone else could do this, it will be "cake" for me. When advised to place my arm into the bucket by the talking head, I plunged my right hand and arm into the ice. The ice and water came about halfway up my forearm. For the first three or four seconds, there was really not a great deal of pain. I found myself thinking in those three or four seconds, "Gee, this is not going to be bad at all!" By the time the sixth or seventh second had passed, I was in excruciating pain. I found myself saying as the pain increased, "Everyone else can do this, I can do this too. I'm going to show these guys I can handle this!" So, I left my hand in the ice. The sixty seconds passed.

The talking head came back on the screen and informed me the sixty seconds was up and I could now remove my hand from the ice. I decided I was going to show them how tough I was and left my arm there for another ten seconds. Then, I lifted a very painful, red, and almost swollen right arm out of the ice. I took the towel, wiped by arm, put it into my lap, and cradled it there until the blood began to run again.

The talking head then said, "Now, Mr. Smith, we are finished with the test. There are some things we need to do here in the other room. Please relax for the next three or four minutes while we complete the calculation of our data."

I was sitting in the chair when the head asked me to relax. I thought, that's fine. I sat there for another three or four minutes waiting for them to finish. At the end of that three or four minutes, a gentleman came in to take all the electrodes off of my body. The tests were completed for the day.

The next morning, I met with my doctor for my consultation. Dr. Booth sat down and spent almost two hours sharing with me the data they had discovered the day before. He proceeded to tell me a fascinating thing. He said, "Mr. Smith, you are one of the coolest reactors we have ever seen." He proceeded to show me on this graph paper how I had reacted under the various stressful situations. Even when the treadmill was in the uphill position and speed had been increased, my cardiovascular system reacted wonderfully. As the stress occurred, my veins and heart didn't overreact. I can remember as I thought about it that I consciously was forcing my heart to do that. It was not something I had been trained to do but something I remember doing.

Then, he showed me what happened when I was in the room with the television monitor. When I went through the pong game, there was no fluctuation whatsoever in the line on the graph that showed my cardiovascular reaction. During the subtraction of the numbers, there was no problem, just cool as a cucumber. When I got to the ice test, I thought I would surely see a rise in my heart rate or some reaction, but it also was just as level as could be.

Then, before turning the next page, he said, "You have a hard time relaxing, don't you?"

I asked him, "What do you mean?"

He turned the page. The only time my cardiovascular system reacted badly in that whole experience was when the talking head on the TV monitor said, "Mr. Smith, we would like you to relax for the next three or four minutes." The second he said relax, the needle in the next room went off the chart. My whole system rejected the idea of relaxing. My heart increased in its rate. My veins constricted. I reacted in all the ways a hot reactor did.

This was a very sobering event for me. My wife has been telling me for years that I need to learn to relax. I have reflected on this a great deal since I took this test. And as I look back over my youth, I remember somehow picking up the idea that productivity and motion were somehow equivalent or related. I can remember feeling that if I was not moving and doing something, that I wasn't of value to anyone or myself. I had completely rejected the idea of relaxing.

For many years, my family didn't take vacations. Vacations were something I didn't consider necessary. I love to work and have always loved to work. It has always been very hard for me to take time off to relax. But since this experience, I have found myself consciously aware of the need in my life to relax, to take the time to stop and smell the roses, to fill my bucket. As my friend Stephen Covey would say, I need time to sharpen my saw.

In the last several years, we made a commitment that we would spend every July as a family on vacation. I can remember the first July we did this. I took the entire month off, and after a week I was a "basket case." I forced myself to go through with it and discovered what a wonderful experience it was to just do things with my family without the pressure of having to do anything related to my business. We have done that every year since.

I find that my weekends are much more exciting and entertaining for me, even though I still find myself moving a great deal when I am at home. For example, we own a ranch now near the little town of Gunlock, Utah. It is a two-thousand-acre ranch with eighteen horses and one hundred cows. There is nothing I enjoy more than going out and working with those animals and cleaning up the ranch. It is a form of relaxation for me. Many people would see it as work, but it is really a form of relaxation for me. And I can return to the ranch house, sit down with my wife or children and just visit without my cardiovascular system rejecting the idea that I am not moving and not being productive.

I believe what really happened to me by going through this testing procedure was that I put a different belief on my belief window. The old belief that I picked up as a child was "productivity and motion are the same. If you're not moving, you're not productive; and if you're not productive, you're not worthwhile."

The new belief is "motion and productivity are not necessarily related. Being busy and productive are not necessarily the same. Relaxing is okay!" I find that since I've adopted this new belief, I'm no longer bound by an external force. I have more control over my life. I can relax and not feel guilty, not feel worthless. The little voice in my head that says "You're worthless if you relax" has been silenced.

Remember, when your self-worth is based on anything outside yourself—by the opinions of others, by material things, or anything else— you're in big trouble over the long run. Feeling good about yourself is an essential ingredient in the recipe for inner peace. The governing values you identified in Section I of this book form the true foundation for healthy self-esteem, and the process of occasionally examining the beliefs that are written on your belief window will help you get rid of self-defeating behaviors.

A great man in my own experience once counseled a group of young men and women, "Be yourself—but be that perfectly." And being your-self perfectly is something we are all capable of doing. Armed with an improving self-image, let's look at our final natural law, Law 10, which deals with one of the great paradoxes of life—the more we give ourselves away, the more we have.

LAW 10

Give more and you'll *have* more

My father was a professor of speech and my mother was a schoolteacher at a local elementary school in the early fifties when we were living in the Hawaiian Islands. We were not doing particularly well financially, a fact which I became aware of when I was older. I discovered, as I looked back on my youth, that we had very little wealth as the world would see it, but we were never poor. I came to realize that there is a big difference between being broke and poor. I have been broke quite often in my life but have never been poor. Poor is a state of mind, but that's another subject altogether.

When I was eight years old, living in the Hawaiian Islands, it appeared that Christmas was going to be pretty lean for our household. My parents were quite concerned about that. They gathered us together in late November or early December to explain to my siblings and me (there were seven of us) that there was not a great deal of money for Christmas. Each of us would have to select one gift that we really wanted, and that one gift would likely be the only one we would receive.

For some reason this is a vivid memory from my youth. I remember giving this a great deal of thought. I came back to my parents and told them that what I really wanted to have was a bushel of apples. I loved apples. I still love them.

My parents were astounded that this was what I wanted for Christmas. They told me they would see what they could do. Apparently, as they tell the story, they went down to the local grocery store on Beretania Street in Honolulu and asked what the price for a bushel of apples would be. In case you're not aware of this, apples don't grow in Hawaii. They have to be shipped in with each apple individually wrapped. This is probably one of the most expensive gifts I could have asked for.

On Christmas morning everyone got up, excited as we always were (and as I still am). The tradition in my family was to line up after eating breakfast and then everyone would walk into the room together to see our gifts from Santa Claus. As I walked into the room I saw over in a corner that had been designated as "my area" the most wonderful bushel of apples I have ever seen. It was in a big box with each apple individually wrapped in yellow tissue paper. I was very excited about that. And as soon as the rest of my family had opened their presents, I grabbed my bushel of apples and went out into the neighborhood to find all my friends. Within a few hours, I had given all of my apples away. I don't remember at the time thinking there was any significance to that. I do remember how wonderful it was to share my apples with all my friends in the neighborhood. The fact that they were gone before sundown was not a problem for me, nor did it occur to me that it could have or should have been a problem.

I suspect that this was my first real experience with the power of the abundance mentality. The abundance mentality is the idea that there is plenty on this planet for everyone. If we will share what we have with each other, everyone can win. This has been a philosophy of mine ever since that Christmas, something I fervently believe in.

Sharing the Wealth

We have never had any trouble creating wealth in this country, or in the world, for that matter. The problem that we have had as human beings is the distribution of that wealth. There have always been people of great wealth and there have always been people living in poverty, not only in this country but all over the world. I have reflected from time to time on what a tragedy that is. Why can't we develop an ability to distribute the wealth as well as we have developed the ability to create it? Steinbeck said it well in his masterpiece, *The Grapes of Wrath*: "Men who can graft the trees and make the seed fertile and big can find no way to let the hungry people eat their produce. Men who have created new fruits in the world cannot create a system whereby their fruits may be eaten. And the failure hangs over the State like a great sorrow."

There are no easy solutions to this dilemma, but I believe that we as individuals can make a difference, if we adopt an abundance mentality. This philosophy, in a nutshell, is this: When individuals accumulate more wealth than they need to live well, the difference between what they spend on living well (everyone has a different definition of living well) and what has been created is really not theirs. This excess wealth is a stewardship that has been given to individuals to take care of and do something with that matters.

For example, if it costs me forty thousand dollars a year to live the way I like to live, and I have developed an ability to generate one hundred thousand dollars annually, after paying Uncle Sam, taking care of any other mandatory expenses, and saving enough to give my family sufficient security for the future, then I have an obligation to share the sixty-thousand-dollar difference, do something with it to alleviate pain, sorrow, and tragedy on the planet.

A number of years ago, I had an opportunity to be in Denver to give a speech. The person who had arranged for me to give that speech was a very wealthy man who lived in an $8 million house. I remember driving by and seeing the house. I was very impressed with what a magnificent, wonderful place it was. But as I flew back to Salt Lake City, I found myself wondering whether this man could get by in a $2 million or maybe a $1.5 million home, take the difference, the $6 million or $6.5 million, and do something with it to alleviate pain and to help those who have not been able to help themselves.

Please do not misunderstand me. I would defend this person's right to own that $8 million house with my life. That is what free enterprise is all about. On the other hand, as I thought about it, I decided that there was a moral issue here. Anyone who has more than he needs has a responsibility to use the excess to help others who have less than they need.

Now, I am not judging this man in Denver. None of us has enough information to judge someone else in this regard. Perhaps this $8 million home represented only a small percentage of his total wealth. I was fairly sure that this was the case. Maybe he had $100 million and was taking $90 million and using it to help others. I have no idea and am not condemning this man at all, but I did wonder if the moral issue had ever occurred to him.

We have an obligation to do something with the difference, and if we do, a natural law of human behavior kicks in and tells us that much good will result. What to do and how to share the difference, however, are much more difficult questions. We have discovered that legislating to do something with the difference does not work. The Communist regimes in the Soviet Union and Europe proved that. We have now seen the complete collapse of Communism. After seventy years of trying to make it work, they finally gave up. They tried to force the distribution of wealth by law. It cannot be done. Instead of creating an abundance, this approach creates a scarcity. We have discovered that in several different areas of the world at different times.

You cannot legislate the distribution of wealth. It has to be done voluntarily. It has to be done by people who want to do it because it is the right thing to do. Do we just give the money away? Probably not. The welfare system has demonstrated that giving money away doesn't work either. We are into the third and fourth generation of welfare people. When people seem to get stuck on welfare they lose their self-esteem. There is no interest in becoming productive. They develop the belief on their belief window that the world somehow owes them a living, and they won't lift their little finger to get the money they are paid. I have real problems with that as well.

So, how is the distribution of the wealth to be accomplished? I wish I had a definitive answer for that. All I am sure of, at this point, is that somehow we have to do it.

Those are pretty easy feelings to have when you don't have a great deal of wealth to distribute. It's easy for someone who is making thirty-five thousand dollars or forty thousand dollars a year to say, "You know, everyone out there who is making one hundred thousand dollars or five hundred thousand dollars should be living on a fifth of that and sharing it somehow with those who are less fortunate."

I've been in that position, and it's easy to have that attitude. The interesting thing for me at this point in my life, though, is that I find myself suddenly in a position where I have created a great deal more wealth than I need. The issue for me now is this: Am I willing to put my wealth where my mouth has been? Happily, I can say that this has not been difficult at all.

There were five of us who initially started the Franklin Quest Company. On one occasion, we met to decide what portion each of us would own. At that time, early 1984, I could have made a good case for why I should have owned a majority of the company. But it didn't occur to me that I should. When the discussion and meeting ended, I had 33 percent. The other partners owned the remaining stock. When the company was created and we decided who would own what percentage, that stock or percentage of ownership was not worth a dime. Today, now that we are a public company, the stock is worth a great deal of money.

As the company grew and we began bringing people on board, we discovered two correct principles: *You can't do everything yourself* and *There really is more than one right way to do something.* This was a revelation to me. We started finding and attracting people into the firm who had the expertise to help us grow and become the corporation that we have become. In fact, there are some wonderful stories, almost eerie, about how specific talent seemed to surface just when we needed it.

It occurred to us then that if people were going to be emotionally involved in the creation and success of Franklin Quest, they should own a piece of the rock. So several years ago, all of the partners decided to give some stock away. We gave the stock away when it was practically worthless to about ten or eleven people who had helped us get Franklin on its feet. As the years went by, we gave other options on the stock so that people would have ownership in what was becoming a wonderful company.

When we finally went public on June 3, 1992, I discovered (I had not really realized this until it was pointed out to me by some of the investment bankers who took us public) that I had given away in gifts and options what now amounted to $36 million. They were amazed that I was willing to do this. It didn't occur to me that this would be amazing to anyone. It simply seemed the right thing to do.

As I reflected on their amazement and on the impact those options have had on the people who received stock, I realized that this was, in fact, proof of the power of the abundance mentality. I said to the investment banker who was amazed that I had given away $36 million of stock,

"If you look at what I gave away in the beginning by not personally taking a majority of the stock, I've given away more than $200 million in stock."

According to today's trading price, the stock I have remaining is worth $60 million. I said to this gentleman, "If I hadn't given away that stock, that ownership in the company, then the ownership I've retained would not be worth anywhere near $60 million. And if you watch our stock over the next few years, I would not be surprised if the stock I have remaining will eclipse all of the stock that I gave away."

He was dumbfounded, and I'm not sure he believed that statement. But I have a firm belief that it's true. What I am worth today, I am worth because I was willing to share the wealth. I believe that is what we have to do in this country. If we find ways to share our excess with others— especially if they prove through hard work, loyalty, creative talent, or even friendship that they deserve a portion of it—that excess will grow faster than if we hoard it for ourselves. This is a natural law. If you want an abundance of anything, the best way to achieve it is by sharing what you have with others. Sharing expands the sense of ownership. Hoarding expands only envy and resentment.

I have an interesting postscript to the apple story here. On June 5, 1992, the SRI Gallup Co. inducted me into their Hall of Fame at a very gracious, black-tie dinner in Lincoln, Nebraska, where their corporate office is located. I have come to know Don Clifton, President and CEO of SRI Gallup, and many of his people as wonderful human beings. At the banquet that evening, Dr. Clifton presented me with a black leather binder that contained eight or ten wonderful letters from people who have made an impact in my life since I was a youth. One of those letters was from my mother, who at that time was in Utah suffering from leukemia. Dr. Clifton read part of that letter to the six hundred people assembled for the award, and, to my surprise, she had included the story about the bushel of apples in Hawaii. After he read the letter and made several nice statements about me and my family, Dr. Clifton presented me with a beautiful bushel of bright red apples. It was quite a moving experience for me. I accepted the apples with more honor than the wonderful plaque they presented to me. The dinner was held after the awards presentation, and I took the apples out and put them on the table where the buffet dinner was being served and shared the apples with all the people present.

Once again, I found myself remembering the experience when I was eight, and I had a reconfirmation of the fact that the abundance mentality is a natural law of the universe. If we will share what we have, many people's lives can be blessed, and what we have left will grow at a geometric rate. I truly believe that. Somehow, not only in this country but all over the world, we need to discover that when we develop more wealth than we need for our own comfort and security, we have an obligation to look at that difference as a stewardship, something to use to bless others. I believe, if everyone who has developed that type of wealth would be willing to look at it as a stewardship, then poverty, suffering, and pain could be greatly reduced, if not eliminated, in the world.

Teaching

The abundance mentality is not limited to finances or other material possessions. This principle can apply to any aspect of our lives where we have been blessed with an abundance. If, for instance, we have obtained through either natural talent or hard work an abundance of knowledge or expertise in a given area, this principle suggests that we should not hoard it, but should share it. This is the principle upon which universities—indeed, our entire education system—are based. Teaching, however, is a bit more complicated than the mere sharing of knowledge.

Teaching has a second purpose: the changing of lives. New knowledge is of little value if it doesn't change us, make us better individuals, and help us to be more productive, happy, and useful. At Franklin Quest we are very serious about this second purpose of teaching. We present thousands of seminars on time management, goal setting, stress management, and other areas that help people gain control of their lives. And in the process we've discovered something important. The teacher has to have an abundance of something more than knowledge to effect change in prospective learners.

As a university student I sat through many lectures where the professor shared his knowledge, but nothing happened in the lives of his students. Something was missing. That something, I believe, is energy. Teaching, in the truest sense of the word, is energy transfer. It's a life force. A teacher whose own life is energized (vibrant and dynamic) can transfer some of that energy to his students, and make them more fully alive.

This is what motivating others is all about. It's a transfer—of knowledge, but more importantly, of energy. The key is that there can be no transfer if the teacher's life is empty. It's like trying to jump-start a car from a dead battery. Again, you can only lift others when you stand on higher ground. You have to have more energy and knowledge than those you are trying to teach, otherwise it is impossible for their lives to change. And the natural law we mentioned above comes into play here. Any effective teacher will tell you that if you share your knowledge with others, the very act of trying to help someone else understand a new concept will increase your own understanding. The teacher generally learns more than the student.

The Servant Leader

There is a great deal of overlap between the role of teacher and the role of leader. In fact, some have said that all great leaders are teachers. Why? Because great leaders motivate people to change, to perform at higher levels. That's what both teaching and leadership are all about. How a true leader accomplishes this, however, ties in directly to the abundance mentality.

If we push the concepts already discussed in this chapter to their logical conclusion, we must ask ourselves what it is that a true leader has an abundance of. A leader may have superior knowledge or an abundance of energy, but I argue that the one asset that sets a genuine leader apart from a cheap imitation is power. True leaders have power. This is not the power of position or wealth or title. It is more the power of influence, which can only be granted by those who choose to be followers. And because a true leader has this power, it is his or her responsibility to share it, in other words, to empower the followers. And, ironically, you cannot empower people unless they have granted you the power to do so. Then wonderful things happen. This, by the way, is the secret to motivating people. You give them back what they have given you, and the result is synergistic. This is what I call servant leadership. It is simply sharing the abundance of power that you have earned by being their servant rather than their master.

I first discovered this principle when I was in the military. You might think this is a strange place to learn about servant leadership, but that's where I learned it. I soon found that I could not motivate people to do anything unless I was in their physical presence. When I was there, they would do what I wanted them to (because of my position at first, not because I was a true leader), but when I was not present, they would do what they wanted to do. This raised a question in my mind. "What is my role as a leader?" I asked myself. And a little light came on in my mind. The answer was simple: My role as a leader was to create an atmosphere in which my people would do what I wanted them to do—even when I wasn't there—*because they wanted to do it*. I had to get them to want what I wanted.

When I got into the army, I opted to go to OCS and receive a commission as an officer. The reason I did that was that I wanted to get married, and my wife's father was not excited about his daughter marrying a private in the army. I managed to graduate with honors, so I had my choice of where I wanted to serve in the military. I selected Pershing missiles and was sent to Germany as a Pershing missile commander. I took over a firing battery, with four nuclear warheads, each one thirty-two times bigger than the Hiroshima bomb. We spent thirty days out of every sixty in the fields of Germany with our missiles pointed in the air, aimed at the Eastern Bloc. We had to have the ability to fire those missiles within twelve minutes of being notified that war had broken out.

When I took over this particular unit, the morale was terrible. The commander I replaced had been a West Pointer, he was in it for life, and he expected everyone to do what he said, no questions, just do it. One problem with his approach to leadership was that the Pershing missile was a very sophisticated weapon, and many of the people who were brought into the Pershing system were college students. We had a pretty bright group and, quite frankly, they liked to question things. They wanted to know why. At any rate, morale was quite low when I arrived, and on one occasion we were out in the field with our missiles, right out in the open where the Russians would drive by in their cars and take pictures of us. Of course we had our guards out at their posts, but they had to stand there in temperatures that would dip well below zero.

I was platoon commander. I had three officers who reported to me, then we had a cluster of noncommissioned officers (sergeants), and finally there were the enlisted men—a typical military hierarchy. And in this structure officers are not supposed to fraternize with the enlisted people. You just don't do that in the military. But I didn't buy into that. While

I was out in the field freezing my fanny off, I said, "You know, we ought to build some guard shacks for these guys." And because we had so much to do, there weren't any enlisted people available to build these guard shacks. We had telephone poles lying in this area, and we had a whole bunch of plywood and two-by-fours. But when I suggested that we build these guys some guard shacks, one of the sergeants looked at me and said, "What do you mean, 'we'?"

I said, "Yeah, let's go build them."

"It's ten below zero out there."

"I don't care how cold it is. Let's go build them."

So I dragged these officers and noncoms out, and we got the telephone poles, cut them off, put them in the ground, and built the first shack. About two in the morning we put the first guard in the shack, and the guards were absolutely dumbfounded at these officers trying to build shacks for them. We put a little heater in the shack and put up some insulation to keep the cold out. The first one was really bad, but the guards thought it was the Taj Mahal. We improved with experience, though, and by six o'clock the next night we had four or five finished and all the guards were standing in guard shacks, off the ground, dry and warm.

Well, word passed through the unit quickly, and the morale started to turn around immediately. Then an interesting thing began to happen. These guards started looking for things to do, and we got our firing time down to six and a half minutes. About three days later we needed to build a latrine. So in typical military fashion a sergeant "volunteered" a private from New York City to dig this latrine. This kid had never had a pick in his hand, but he started whacking the ground with it anyway, and it soon became obvious that it was going to take him approximately forever.

I said to him, "Have you ever had a pick in your hand before?"

He said, "Oh, sure, I've had a pick in my hand."

"Well," I said, "let me show you how to use it."

So I took the pick from him and dug about half the latrine. About ten minutes into this we had fifteen guys standing around the edge of this hole watching us. They were absolutely blown away. I had taken my shirt off, so I was just in my T-shirt, and I was having a great time showing this kid how to use a pick. By the time we finished this little lesson, he really did know how to use a pick.

On that particular day some officers from another unit were there, and one of them was a captain. "You took your shirt off," he said. "Why did you do that?"

"Why did I take my shirt off? You can't dig a trench with a shirt on," I said.

"How's anybody going to know that you're an officer without your shirt on?"

I looked at him and said, "You know, if I have to wear that crummy bar on my lapel so that people will know I'm an officer, then I've got a real problem."

This guy missed the whole point. In his mind, the only way he was able to show his authority was by a small insignia. And in my opinion, if that's the only way you can let your people know you've got authority, you've lost. They're not going to follow you anywhere. What a leader does is get people to do things because they want to, not because they have to. Digging that latrine trench and building those guard shacks made a difference and the morale turned around, because of the message sent by the actions. They got the message loud and clear that the people at the top cared about the people at the bottom of the traditional military hierarchy. We were willing to get physically involved in doing something for them, and they then decided to return the favor. The real lesson I learned from this experience is that if you take care of the people below you, they'll take care of you. And that's important, because your success is dependent on the success of the people under you.

In the 56th Artillery Group in Germany, which had all the Pershing missiles, there were four battalions. The group had a need for a headquarters battery commander. Supposedly, you had to be a major to fill this slot. But the group commander, as a result of what we had done in inspiring the men out in the field, promoted me to headquarters battery commander. There I was, a first lieutenant in a major's slot. I was excited. But the group's morale was terrible. Part of the problem was the living conditions for the rank and file soldiers. They lived in a building that had been the headquarters for Field Marshal Rommel during World War II. It was a six-story building, and apparently nothing in it had been renovated since Rommel died in 1944. The walls were falling in and it was an ugly place.

When I first took over, I said, "This place is in terrible shape. We've got to fix it up." I asked one of my men what we could do about it. He said, "Well, we can put in a requisition to the Corps of Engineers, and they will do anything we want them to do, but it will take at least four years to make it happen." I asked him if there were any other alternatives. "Maybe we can get the German nationals to come in and do it, but we'd have to pay them, and we don't have any money."

"Will they take anything else?"

"Well," he said, "they'll take stuff."

"What kind of stuff?"

"They'll take plywood, and they'll take coffee."

I said, "Well, let's get the stuff."

"No," he answered, "none of that stuff is available. You can't get it." And he had all these reasons why we couldn't do this thing.

This happened about the time the French refused to let the Americans operate from bases in France. They gave the military three weeks to dismantle all their equipment and get it out of France. Because they had to move so fast, a lot of stuff was being thrown away. I heard about this from one of my warrant officers, a guy named Chief Hewlett. "You know," he said, "I know what we need to get this place fixed up. But we've got to go to France to do it."

"Do you know where it is?" I said.

"Yeah, but you know it's against regulations to use our vehicles like this."

"What do you need?" I said.

"I need five five-ton trucks."

We had these big extra-long, five-ton trucks that had equipment on them. So we took the equipment off these trucks, which means that if we had been caught, we would have been in deep yogurt. I selected ten men, two for each truck, and I said, "You guys be back in three days. I can cover for you for three days." So they took off for France, they went to all these bases, and three days later at 2 A.M. five 5-ton trucks rolled in, loaded to the gills. You wouldn't believe the stuff. There were two trucks full of three-quarter-inch plywood, which in Germany was like gold, half a truckload of ten-pound cans of coffee, and all kinds of typewriters. And on one truck they had twelve big, gorgeous, leather-stuffed general officer chairs. I didn't dare ask where they found them. And we stored all this stuff in the basement.

Then we went to the German nationals and showed them what we wanted done to the building. And the Germans said, "Yeah, we can do this. What will you give us?" And we showed them the plywood. They came in and started in the basement, completely sandblasted the walls, restuccoed, put in fluorescent lights, painted the floor, and it looked like a mansion when we finished.

When the guys in this unit started seeing all the changes, the morale shot up immediately. Then we went to where these guys lived and turned the Germans loose. They sanded the oak floors, restuccoed the walls, bordered the walls with stained plywood, and these guys thought they were living in a palace. We got new beds for them, new everything. It got to the point where these guys wouldn't even walk on their floors with their shoes. They'd walk through the door and take their boots off, because they didn't want to hurt their room.

And you should have seen my office. Have you ever heard of a first lieutenant with a general officer chair? It was incredible. But the last thing we did was the mess hall. I said, "I want this to look like a restaurant." So we completely redid the floor, restuccoed all the walls, got a picture of the Tetons that was thirteen feet long and eight feet high, and hung it. We got new tables, new chairs, put tablecloths and candles on the tables. It took about a week to do this. And word got out all over Europe. We had general officers flying in helicopters to eat at our restaurant. We kept this a big secret from the men while the remodeling was going on, and the first time they saw it, they were absolutely amazed.

And do you know what resulted from all this? I had steak every single night when I was in the field. I don't know where they got the steak, but the mess sergeant said to me, "Hey you've taken care of me, I'm going to take care of you." But more important was how this unit performed. We were supposed to be able to mobilize in two hours in case of war. When I got there, they could have done it in maybe three days. But after the remodeling, the men took such pride in themselves and their unit that we could be in the field forty-five minutes after getting orders to move. And it was incredible how fast the whole situation turned around. This, because we decided that we as officers needed to be servants of our people.

Our group commander, Colonel Powers, had been requisitioning a fancy metal command post for two years and couldn't get one. Well, we found two of these things in France, and we hooked both together so that they made a fairly good sized room. Then we set it up out on the parade field, and when Col. Powers saw his new command post, he walked over to it and wept. "Where did you get this?" he said.

"I don't know," I answered. And from that moment on, I could do no wrong with my commanding officer. He came into my office and saw the general officer's chair and said, "Hey, where did you get that chair?"

"Just don't ask. You want one?"

He said, "I'd kill for a chair like that."

We had it in his office in twenty minutes. He was just blown away.

The main point is this: When I'm given a little authority, yes, I can exercise dominion over you if I want to, but that just doesn't work. You don't get results by lording it over people. The magic about the servant-leader idea is that we could give people orders and they would feel like they had been *asked*.

Col. Powers caught onto this idea. One day several general officers came to visit, and one of them ended up in the office of Sgt. Major "Rip" Van Winkle. Sgt. Major Van Winkle had been in the army forever—I think he must have been at Valley Forge—and he understood what the colonel and I understood about leadership. Well, one of these generals came in and sat on Van Winkle's desk, and the sgt. major said, "Sir, get your ass off my desk."

The general looked at him and said, "Are you sure?"

And Van Winkle said, "Sir, I want you to get your ass off my desk."

The general walked into Col. Powers's office and said, "Colonel, your sergeant major just told me to get my ass off his desk. What are you going to do about that?"

Col. Powers looked at Sgt. Major Van Winkle and said, "Did you tell the general to get his ass off your desk?"

"Yes sir, I did."

Well, Col. Powers turned to the general and said, "Get your ass off his desk."

You can imagine how Van Winkle felt about Col. Powers. And more important, you can imagine how he felt about himself. There is a causal relationship between self-worth and productivity, as we discussed in an earlier chapter, and there is nothing that makes people feel greater self-worth than having leaders who go out of their way to serve them. In short, if you want to get greater productivity out of people, serve them, don't exercise dominion over them.

All managers have one type of authority through their positions. But that authority is largely ineffective if it is used to manipulate and push people. No one who uses authority in this manner has an abundance of power. Servant leaders, on the other hand, may not even have the authority of position, but they will have an abundance of real power, real influence with people, because they have earned it. Their followers have given it to them. When you are trusted with that kind of power, you have an obligation to share it, to empower others.

One thing we need to remember as we consider the issue of power is that when people grant us power and we have developed the ability to lead, leadership becomes a two-edged sword. A statement I heard a long time ago—I'm not sure where—which has had a great impact on me is as follows: *The power to lead is the power to mislead. The power to mislead is the power to destroy.*

As leadership skills are developed and strengthened, we must remember that leadership can also be used for evil. Hitler was probably one of the greatest leaders the world has ever seen, but he used that leadership ability to destroy. George Washington was also a magnificent leader. He used his leadership ability to build, lift, and create. Leadership carries with it a great responsibility—the responsibility to lift others, to empower them to do more with their lives than they otherwise would be able to. That is the mark of a true leader, one who understands the abundance mentality.

Equality through Abundance

Equality is a value we embrace in America. "We hold these Truths to be self-evident," said Jefferson in the Declaration of Independence, "that all Men are created equal, that they are endowed by their Creator with certain unalienable Rights, that among these are Life, Liberty, and the pursuit of Happiness." These rights, we say, are for everyone, not just the privileged few. We don't believe that some people are more deserving of a good life than others. We want everyone to have a good life. Equality, in this sense, is something we firmly believe in.

And the abundance mentality is a great equalizing force, even though it is a completely free method of leveling the human playing field. In this sense, it is the exact opposite of Communism, which tries to force an artificial equality on people. The abundance mentality tries instead to *lift* everyone to new levels. We sometimes think, because our society has grown self-centered and selfish in recent years, that the purpose of freedom and democracy is to allow us to seek abundance for ourselves alone, to raise ourselves above the masses. But that is not the case at all. Our American system was set up in such a way that individuals *can* obtain an abundance, but with that privilege comes an obligation to seek the improvement of the entire society. If we focus on the privilege and forget our obligation, the system breaks down. That's why it isn't working today. We've neglected the abundance mentality. We've forgotten how to share, how to lift each other.

You might be wondering what the abundance mentality and servant leadership have to do with the Reality Model and gaining control of your life. To me, the powerful natural law of giving of ourselves and, in the process, finding that we have everything we really want and need, is one of the great secrets of life. And, of all the beliefs we can have on our belief windows, this is among the most profound in our quest for inner peace.

I know that it seems to run counter to everything that common sense and human nature appear to tell us. But, to me, that is part of the wonder of the idea, and a reminder to me that in the midst of the weaknesses and selfishness and inhumanity of the human race, there is also a nobler, diviner side. Something of the divine exists in all of us, and as we respond to that inner light and unselfishly share our talents and means with others, that light will grow and spread to others. All but the basest of human beings can be touched by kindness and generosity, when selflessly offered. And for those who do the giving, what is received in return is the greatest gift of all—inner peace.

Give, and it will be given to you; good measure, pressed down, shaken together, running over, they pour into your lap. For by your standard of measure it will be measured to you in return.

—Luke 6:38

CONCLUSION

Putting It All Together

Well, we've reached the end of this learning experience. If you've stayed with me this far you've seen that the process of examining your inner values and beliefs is not easy, nor is it necessarily pleasant. When I first went through this process, it was tough to describe in words so many things that I had previously been aware of only at a feeling level. And some of the beliefs on my belief window, when brought to the light of day and examined, were positively scary. Yet, coming to a conscious awareness of what was really important to me was one of the watershed experiences of my life. Then, as I built my Productivity Pyramid and began to apply the principles of value-based event control, I started to experience the inner peace we all seek. In the same way, using the Reality Model to understand how the things written on my belief window were both helping and hindering me in my continuing quest for inner peace was a pivotal and soul-enlarging experience.

As you've gone through the material and the exercises in Part II, you may not have been aware of the close relationship between the Reality Model and the Productivity Pyramid. In fact, the two models are visual representations of the same process. You can see the parallels in the

213

comparative drawings below. So that the elements line up properly, we have tipped the Reality Model on end.

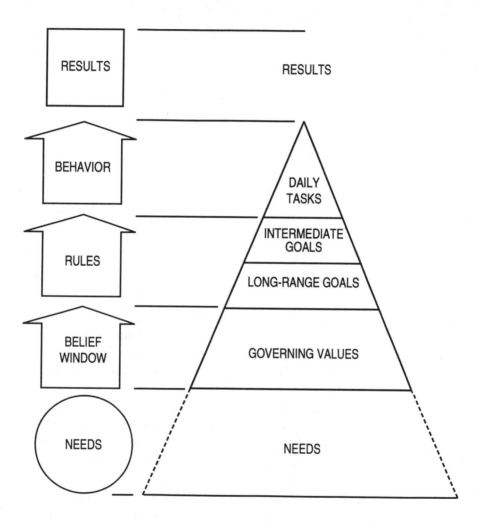

Note that the Needs Wheel represents a level of consciousness that lies below the Governing Values level of the pyramid. In the Productivity Pyramid this would be the level we'd find if we excavated a bit deeper at its base. Likewise, the Results box of the Reality Model represents a level above the pyramid that is only implied, but there nevertheless. The other elements correspond as shown: Governing Values are numbered among the things on your Belief Window, the Long-range Goals and Intermediate Goals are only a conscious form of the Rules you set up as a result of your Governing Values, and Daily Tasks are a part of your here-and-now daily Behavior.

As you can see, the Reality Model deals with a much broader slice of your life, whereas the Productivity Pyramid focuses more narrowly on the process of how we get things done. But both models are indispensible tools in helping us achieve the larger goal of inner peace. You can use the Reality Model to help identify your deeper values and motivations, and it can help you identify and change beliefs that don't seem to be working or are obviously not reflective of reality. Then use the powerful processes of the Productivity Pyramid to organize those values and motivations into a systematic program for implementing them in your daily life. Instead of letting your subconscious translate your values and beliefs into rules and goals, you take over to consciously describe them as long-range and intermediate goals and daily tasks that can be systematically achieved.

Before we conclude things, I'd like to give you one additional bit of food for thought. If you've been reading between the lines, you have already noted that inner peace seems to come from getting certain things in line with each other. In Part I, I stressed that our daily tasks need to be in line with (reflective of) our governing values if we are to experience inner peace. In Part II, we learned that not only must our behavior be in line with (meeting) our needs, but that the beliefs we have placed on our belief window must be in line with reality (truth, or things as they really are). If our beliefs are not rooted in reality, our consequent behavior will produce frustration and anything but inner peace. When our beliefs are congruent with truth and natural law, we really do experience inner peace.

But I believe there is one other ingredient that needs to line up with all these things we've talked about if we are to experience the most fulfilling type of inner peace. Everything we've talked about—our governing values, daily tasks, beliefs based on natural law, and behavior—must line up with *moral* truth. By that I mean whatever set of moral beliefs you have, your most deeply held inner convictions about life, its meaning, and how we as human beings and/or a higher power expect us to conduct ourselves in our relationships as part of the human race. I'm purposely leaving a more precise description of moral truth to you, and I'm not necessarily talking about organized religious beliefs. Even the most ardent atheist still holds some inner convictions about who we are and how we should treat each other. Whatever those convictions are for you, it's important that all we have talked about be congruent with them if you are to find the deepest and most satisfying form of inner peace.

This deeply held belief on my part came to full realization several years ago when I was teaching our time management seminar to a group of Baptists in Atlanta. We had reached the point in the seminar where I had taught the group about the Productivity Pyramid. We had covered governing values, long-range and intermediate goals, and were talking about how they could do something about their governing values on a daily basis.

We took a break and during that time one of the participants in the seminar approached me and said, "You know, Hyrum, the stuff you are teaching comes right out of the Bible." When he said that, I thought perhaps I had offended him. I asked, "What do you mean by that?" He said, "Well, I am very excited about this concept. The idea of value-based goal setting goes back a long way. It sounds like the kinds of things that come out of the Bible."

Discovering that he was not offended, I opened up. I asked, "Would you like to hear my personal conviction?"

He said, "Yes, I would."

"Well, in the seminar we teach that we must bring together two elements in order to have inner peace. One of those elements is the identification of our governing values, what really matters to us. The other is bringing our performance, event control if you will, controlling the events of our lives, in line with those values. When those two line up, we experience this feeling of inner peace." Then I said, "In my opinion, there really is a third element that has to be brought in line for the ultimate inner peace."

He asked, "Really, what's that?"

I answered, "It's absolute moral truth. When we bring our values in line with moral truth and then bring our performance in line with that, we will experience the ultimate kind of inner peace."

He got pretty excited about that idea and stated, "You've got to share that with this group." I was hesitant about it, but he reassured me that this particular group would appreciate the additional insights this concept provides. I did share my feelings with the group, and we had a wonderful discussion about things that really mattered a lot in all of our lives.

Only a rare few ever seem to find this ultimate kind of inner peace. We've probably all known one or two such people, and some of the more widely known individuals who seem to possess it have found themselves among the most respected and honored people of our time. And besides the Mother Theresas, you probably know or know of many "ordinary" persons who just seem to have it all together in the inner spiritual sense. These people are not always the famous ones; more often they are those we recognize as simply "good" people—and that "goodness" shines through from something calm and radiant deep within. My own experiences have shown me that, to some degree, all of us can come to a unity of inner values, things written on our belief windows, daily actions, and understanding of moral truth that can produce a kind of inner peace that transcends anything we can imagine. I encourage you as part of your quest for inner peace to do a real search to identify the fundamental moral truths that are available to us from many sources. The source of those laws doesn't really matter; all that matters is that you experiment with them, find those that are true natural laws, live by them, and witness that they actually work. In the process of doing that, I believe that you will come closer to ultimate inner peace.

One other bit of advice as you embark on your own personal quest: At the end of each day or the beginning of the following day, take time to measure the results. Was my behavior in line with my governing values? Did I do what really mattered to me today? Start the cycle over every single day. Take control of your life by implementing the natural laws and concepts we have talked about. Look at the beliefs you've placed on your belief window. Take the ones off that don't work. Identify more correct ones. Burn them indelibly onto your belief window in the form of governing values. Search for the great moral truths that can form the inner compass for your effort.

Then, do something about it. Set some meaningful and worthwhile goals. Further them through your actions on a daily basis. When you are willing to do these things, you will have taken complete control of your own life, your own destiny, and you will have a right to this magnificent thing that no one can take away from you called inner peace.

ENDNOTE

About Franklin Quest Co.

When we created the first Franklin Day Planner and started teaching seminars back in late 1983, I didn't have an inkling of what it would grow into a decade later. Today, more than two million people use the Franklin Day Planner, and that number grows each month as more people attend one of our seminars or purchase Day Planners, binders, accessories, and books at Franklin retail stores in major metropolitan areas across America.

The Franklin Day Planner, originally available only in a 5½ × 8½ inch page size, is now produced in four sizes, including the traditional Classic size, the Pocket (3½ × 6 inches), the Compact (4¼ × 6¾ inches), and the Monarch size (with 8½ × 11 inch pages). An electronic version of the Franklin Time Management System is also available to users of IBM-compatible and Macintosh personal computers through $Ascend_{TM}$, a powerful personal information manager software program that can print to and be used in combination with the printed Franklin Planner.

Training in the Franklin Time Management System is available through open enrollment public seminars held in nearly two hundred cities, as well as seminars geared specifically for corporate, government, nonprofit, and educational organizations. Franklin's corps of professional training consultants are among the best in the business. And, in addition to our flagship Time Management seminar, Franklin Quest also offers other seminars that address topics such as the use of the Franklin system in reducing stress, managing projects more effectively, and improving sales techniques.

For more information about Franklin Quest seminars and products, or to receive a free catalog, call toll-free 1-800-654-1776; or write to P.O. Box 25127, Salt Lake City, Utah 84125-0127.